Your Rights at Work

FIFTH EDITION

Your Rights at Work

Everything you need to know about starting a job, time off, pay, problems at work – and much more

a *TUC* guide

KoganPage

LONDON PHILADELPHIA NEW DELHI

First published in 2000
Second edition 2004
Third edition 2008
Fourth edition 2012
Fifth edition 2016

2nd Floor, 45 Gee Street
London
EC1V 3RS
United Kingdom

© Trades Union Congress (TUC) 2016

The TUC thanks Simpson Millar Solicitors for its help in updating many parts of this edition.

ISBN   978 0 7494 7603 8
E-ISBN   978 0 7494 7607 6

British Library Cataloguing-in-Publication Data

A CIP record for this book is available from the British Library.

Typeset by Graphicraft Limited, Hong Kong
Print production managed by Jellyfish
Printed and bound in Great Britain by CPI Group (UK) Ltd, Croydon CR0 4YY

Contents

Foreword

Few people will go through their working life without needing to know something about employment law. That is not to say that most workplaces are full of abuse or exploitation. They're not. Most employers aim to treat their staff fairly, and most succeed most of the time. But, even in the best-run organizations, things can go wrong.

That does not mean that anyone's first instinct should be to go to court or call a lawyer. It's usually best not to use legal procedures unless all else fails. The law is important because it sets basic standards that no employer can fall below. It gives good employers a starting point on which they can do better, and many do indeed offer contractual rights that are better than the law requires.

Even in non-union workplaces it is generally best to try to resolve issues informally. The knowledge from this book will give you the confidence to make the arguments that can help resolve an issue.

This book is not a hard sell for union membership, and we have tried to make it useful whether or not you are a union member, or whether or not unions are recognized in your workplace.

But the one advantage of a unionized workplace is that there are likely to be proper procedures for resolving difficult issues. If someone is suffering bullying or harassment, someone will already have worked out what can be done to try to resolve the issue.

In recent years basic legal rights in the workplace have improved. Everyone now takes the national minimum wage for granted, but it is not that old. We were one of the last advanced countries to introduce this basic right, and it was controversial to the last, with some who said it would lead to big job losses. Now we have minimum pension rights too as people are auto-enrolled into a pension to which their employer has to contribute.

Unions have been strong campaigners for these new rights at work, persuading government to legislate for a range of advances.

We now have holiday rights, shared parental leave, rights for part-timers, an end to discrimination based on age, sexuality or religion, and rights for agency workers.

But as we produce the fifth edition of *Your Rights at Work* the advance of casualization, short-term contracts and zero-hours working is leaving thousands of workers more in need of protection than ever before.

Almost every advance in employment rights has been opposed by at least some employers and those on the political right. We are told it will be bad for the economy and cause needless 'red tape'.

We can go back to the 19th century and find similar arguments made against laws that prevented children working – and sometimes dying – as chimney sweeps. Lord Lauderdale told the House of Lords when opposing such a law that change 'should be left entirely to the moral feelings of perhaps the most moral people on the face of the earth'. But unfortunately we have learnt through the years that not every UK employer would win a global morality contest.

The argument that stripping away rights is good for the economy fails to stand up. Even after the welcome reforms of recent years, the United Kingdom comes low down the international league table for rights at work. Countries with much better standards have higher standards of living and fewer people unemployed. Our country is still badly damaged by the banking crisis of 2008, and wages growth has been slowed to levels not seen since Victorian times, but it is absurd to think that making it easier to sack people or reducing maternity leave is the route to economic prosperity.

But it is not all bad news. Even this government has improved some rights at work. Sometimes this is because European law has forced them to against their wishes, but on other issues such as ending statutory retirement ages or improving the right to request flexible working they have done better than previous governments – and on pensions auto-enrolment they have achieved what they have promised.

It is important to understand what this book is and what it isn't. Our purpose is to provide a general introduction to your rights at work, but it is not a legal textbook. To keep things relatively clear we have had to simplify some issues. We have not covered some situations or exemptions that affect only a very few people at work.

You cannot rely on this book therefore as expert legal advice that automatically covers your situation. What it aims to do is explain the general requirements of the law in a way that can tell anyone with a problem whether it is worth taking further advice.

One difference between the first and later editions of this book is that we have now re-launched workSMART, the TUC world of work website. This contains up-to-date information not just on employment rights but on health and safety and pensions as well. For those wanting to join a union, it also features a union finder that can help identify the most appropriate union. You can find workSMART at **www.worksmart.org.uk**.

Throughout the book you will find some case studies of tribunal and court hearings. These are based on real cases, and employment law experts will no doubt recognize some of them. We have, however, simplified them where necessary, and changed some of the names involved. You will also find references to amounts of money, such as the current level of the minimum wage or the earnings limit for National Insurance contributions. The figures given are for 2016, but may well have been uprated by the time you read this. Normally, figures go up a few per cent a year, often in line with inflation.

Many TUC staff have contributed to the five editions of this book over the years, and they are too numerous to thank individually, but in particular I would like to record the work of Linda Stewart, Partner and Head of Employment Law at Simpson Millar LLP, who has once again updated many parts of the text.

Frances O'Grady
TUC General Secretary

Introduction

Your basic rights

Everyone at work is protected by a series of basic legal rights – some old and some new. Some protect you against the worst kinds of exploitation and unfair treatment. Some give you positive rights that provide some choice, and some voice, in your working life. And some are there to ensure that your employer keeps their side of the basic bargain at the heart of any job – you work and in return you get paid and receive other benefits.

Most large employers are careful that their general employment practices stay within the law. If your employer is large enough to have a dedicated personnel or human resources section, they should have the expertise that ensures they know their legal obligations. But that does not mean that everyone in the organization will always follow company policy. And in any case there are still good and bad large employers.

Many offer terms and conditions well above the legal minimum. They know that treating their staff well and giving them a real say in the way they do their work make for a more productive workforce. Others, particularly many of those offering low-paid or insecure jobs, may simply want to stay just on the right side of the law. These are the employers who describe the most modest advances in employee rights as red tape and burdens on business.

Many small firms are good employers. Small business organizations often say that their staff are treated like part of the family. This is no doubt true in the best organizations, even if not every family is always a picture of perfect happiness. But others are not good employers. Sometimes this is because they depend on low wages and poor-quality working conditions for the success of their business. In Britain today there are still sweatshops that Dickens would recognize.

Many more get into difficulties simply because they do not know their legal obligations as employers, or do not know how to respond to a difficult situation. Even though employment tribunals do not expect them to have the same formal procedures as large firms, small businesses often end up losing cases because they simply do not have any procedures for resolving disputes or problems at work, or know how to set them up if needed. This, though, is no excuse, and all employers are obliged to have basic procedures in place.

Issues covered by the law

Even in the best-run organizations things can go wrong. You can end up being bullied by your manager even though your employer has an anti-bullying policy. It may be that the behaviour of one of your colleagues would be considered harassment. Even in organizations with good health and safety records, you may be the unlucky one who does have a bad accident. And work-related stress is on the increase everywhere.

Rapid economic change has led to many people being made redundant or being forced to accept insecure jobs such as zero-hours contracts. Even if you are young and skilled and live in South-East England, you may still find it difficult to find and remain in work when you're having to compete with older, more experienced individuals. For older employees redundancy can be devastating. Many jobs have always been insecure, but fewer and fewer jobs can now be said to be secure for life.

You may be falsely accused of wrongdoing, or a minor infringement of rules may be blown up into an excuse to dismiss you. You may be tempted to walk away, but you will still need a reference.

Becoming a parent probably puts more strain on your working life than anything else. Maternity leave, paternity leave and new rights to shared parental leave are designed to support you in the workplace through the transition to parenthood.

Finding a proper balance between work and the rest of your life can be an issue. British workers work the longest hours in Europe. Some need the overtime. But many office workers who do not get overtime are trapped in an increasingly US-style long-hours culture – leaving work before your manager (even if you have worked productively) is taken as indicating a lack of commitment.

Discrimination may not be as overt as it once was but it still exists in Britain's workplaces. Candidates with names suggesting a black or ethnic minority background are much less likely to be shortlisted for jobs than those with names suggesting a white background. Men are still paid more than women for equal work. Some disabled workers face enormous difficulties getting a job despite duties on employers to make adjustments to put them on an equal footing. Lesbian, gay, bisexual and people are more than twice as likely to report being bullied at work as heterosexual employees.

All of these are issues where the law may be able to help you, or where you need to know what the law says. Everyone at work should have a basic knowledge of employment law.

What you might get from legal action

Not every employment dispute will, or should, end up in an employment tribunal or court or require lawyers to get involved. Every so often you may read in the papers of a case where someone has won, if not quite a lottery-sized payout, then at least a substantial amount of money. But these cases are very much the exception. Awards of compensation are normally much smaller, and going to court, even the more informal employment tribunals that hear many work-related cases, can still be traumatic and expensive: it now costs money simply to lodge an application with a tribunal. If you need to buy your own legal advice, it can also be expensive; there is no legal aid for representation at employment tribunals, and since 2013 getting legal aid to pursue employment claims has become much harder and is restricted to claims involving discrimination only.

This book is not, therefore, about how to win a jackpot at an employment tribunal – you probably have more chance with a lottery ticket. Nor does it advise that you should always take legal action when resolving problems at work. In most circumstances, except perhaps when you have lost your job, legal action should always be seen as a last resort. But a simple knowledge of where you stand legally can often help resolve issues informally at an early stage. Simply dropping a hint that you are thinking of getting advice about early stages of repetitive strain injury (RSI) can often be an effective way of getting a better chair and workstation. In general, letting your employer know that you have rights can often lead to a swift improvement, particularly if your employer is ignorant of the law.

Unions and employment rights

Resolving disputes is normally much easier in workplaces where unions are recognized. Nearly every basic recognition agreement between a union and an employer will have ways of resolving both individual and collective grievances. There will be proper procedures for dealing with disciplinary issues. This is sensible for both employers and employees. Companies, these days, are fond of asserting in their annual reports that their staff are their greatest asset. Ensuring staff have ways of raising problems with a real expectation that they will be solved is one relatively modest way of demonstrating that in practice.

Reading some newspapers, you might conclude that unions are quick to bring tribunal cases. In fact the opposite is true. Most tribunal cases come from non-unionized companies, particularly small businesses. This is because they often do not have the kind of procedures needed to ensure that disputes and grievances can be settled properly in-house, or are ignorant of such basic employee protection as not being able to sack someone because she is pregnant.

How to raise an issue

It can be much more difficult to raise an issue in a non-union workplace. While you do have legal rights that can be enforced, it does not mean that this will be easy. The employment relationship is one-sided. Your employer may treat you badly because you've raised a problem. On the other hand, it may be that your employer was completely unaware of the problem and is happy to deal with it informally. You must make your own judgement about how, or even whether, you raise an issue.

If you are not the only one with a grievance, there is strength in numbers. You and your colleagues should consider joining a union. There are rights that allow union officers to represent you with your employer, even if they do not recognize a union, and if there is sufficient support they must recognize and deal properly with your union (see Chapter 5).

Sometimes round-robin e-mails or petitions have persuaded an employer that there is widespread dissatisfaction and they need to take action. In other cases an anonymous letter that includes a government publication making it clear that the employer could be acting unlawfully can bring about change. You might think about sending a delegation to your employer, with very clear backing from the rest of the workforce. Some issues – such as the minimum wage or health and safety issues – can be discussed with an official body outside the workplace, and it can raise problems on your behalf with the employer without revealing who tipped it off in the first place.

If the worst comes to the worst you may be able to walk out of your job and claim what is known as 'constructive dismissal'. In other words, you persuade an employment tribunal that your employer has behaved so badly as to breach your contract, leaving you no option but to resign. However, these claims are quite difficult to win and you should read Chapter 7 carefully and take further advice before resigning. But of course, if your employer has already sacked you unfairly, you may have little to lose by taking action.

Even if you take an action and win, it may still be an unpleasant and difficult experience. While many tribunal cases are over quickly, some can drag out or end up going through lengthy appeal stages. You may end up being cross-examined by an aggressive lawyer for your employer with the aim of showing you in the worst possible light. If it's a case with a media angle, this could be reported in the papers.

The TUC believes people should stand up for their rights. Bad employers do need tackling. A long and difficult case may end up clarifying the law, and thus help thousands of other people. But you should be aware of both the potential benefits *and* the downsides of taking any action. You should always talk this through very carefully with an adviser before committing yourself to a course of action that could bring you into conflict with your employer.

As well as trade unions, there are many other advice agencies that may be able to help, such as your local Citizens Advice Bureau or law centre. There is a range of telephone helplines – some run by voluntary groups set up to deal with particular problems and others by official or publicly funded groups, such as Acas. The TUC has its own workSMART website, **www.worksmart.org.uk**, which provides up-to-date information on employment rights and can point you in the right direction if you want to know which union you should join. These resources are all listed in Chapter 9.

Employment law

In a book like this, we can provide only a general introduction to employment law. Inevitably we have had to simplify many issues. The law may even have changed since this book was written. As we will stress many times, you always need to take detailed advice about your particular circumstances. The rest of this chapter gives a basic introduction to your rights at work and explains some of the key concepts in employment law.

The first important thing to understand is the difference between an employee and a worker. In everyday conversation employee is probably just a slightly posh term for a worker, but in law they are quite different concepts. Employees have many more rights than workers. To understand the difference, you need to understand the nature of the contract between you and your employer, which we explain on pages 10–12.

There are two different kinds of right. There is a basic floor of legal protection that every employee enjoys. In addition, because there is a contract between you and your employer – you work and in return they pay you – you may have additional rights provided by this contract.

The law does not just protect you from a bad or unfair employer; it also imposes duties on you and allows your employer to take action against you if you are guilty of misconduct.

Statutory rights

The basic rights that provide a minimum floor for everyone derive from the law of the land and are known as statutory rights. These normally come either from a government initiative, like the minimum wage, or from Europe, like the Working Time Directive.

The employment rights such as unpaid parental leave that come from Europe are the result of negotiations between employers and unions at the European level. But the European directives that result from this process are turned into UK law. This will normally be done through a set of legally binding regulations.

While parliament makes new laws, the courts have to interpret them. Although laws are intended to be precise, they can never cover every eventuality. Inevitably they will contain words that are a matter of opinion; for example, 'reasonable' is frequently found in employment law, and an employer's definition of reasonable may not be the same as that of an employee they have just sacked. Over time the courts will hear enough cases that require them to decide how to apply words like 'reasonable' for a body of what lawyers call 'case law' to develop. This makes it much easier to predict how a case will go when it gets to court, as normally the courts will want to make decisions in line with previous similar cases. Sometimes, however, a particular case will set an important new legal precedent, and will end up going through every possible appeal stage (see Chapter 8).

For some employment laws that are relatively new there won't be many court cases. It is sometimes hard, therefore, to give precise guidance on how some new rights will be interpreted by the courts. And, while the legal system is heavily based on case law, sometimes the courts can be persuaded to look again at an issue.

Another legal route sometimes used in employment law challenges whether the government has properly put European directives into UK law. European directives are often quite broadly drawn because they need to apply across the countries that make up the European Union, with all their different legal systems and industrial relations traditions. While there is usually room for flexibility in some areas, sometimes a case will be brought using the argument that the UK government has not properly implemented a European directive. (This book goes to press just before the referendum on the UK's membership of the EU. If the UK leaves the EU, the obligation to obey these directives may be thrown into doubt.)

Such cases can end up in the European Court of Justice – the European Union's court where European law is normally settled. An example of this process includes the question of what must be included in the calculation of holiday pay under the Working Time Regulations. Pilots' union BALPA brought the case of *Williams v British Airways ECJ C155/10* in the European Court of Justice. The court ruled that payments which are 'intrinsically linked' to the job and paid as part of normal salary should be included. Employers must now include sales commission, travel time payments, shift or weekend premium payments and anti-social hours payments as well as certain types of overtime when calculating holiday pay.

Contractual rights

The second type of employment rights you enjoy is called contractual rights, so termed because they flow from the contract between you and your employer. Your employment contract is a personal, legal agreement that governs your relationship with your employer.

Employment contracts are usually written down, and you will normally be given one before or when you start work. But even if you are not given a written contract the courts will rule that a contract exists simply because you are being paid in return for working. Whether written or not, your contract will oblige your employer to pay you for work or services performed, to provide work for you, to provide a safe working environment and to behave in a 'reasonable' manner.

You are obliged to 'serve' (or to work or perform a service personally), to be 'obedient', to be competent and careful and to act in good faith. These old-fashioned terms are still used in the courts. They are called 'implied' terms, because they are not necessarily written into the contract but are assumed by the courts to exist in any relationship between an employer and an employee or worker.

If you have a written contract, it will also include other terms that regulate the relationship you have with your employer. It is likely to include how much you will be paid, what notice of dismissal your employer must give you, and your entitlement to holidays. Because they are written down, unlike the implied terms, they are called 'express' terms.

Although these express terms are in addition to your statutory rights, they do impact on your more general legal rights. This is because they define the kind of employment relationship you have with your employer. As the next section explains, there are different types of relationship between employer and employed, and each carries different entitlements to statutory rights.

Worker or employee?

Whether you are a worker or an employee depends upon the contractual relationship you have with your employer.

If your employer provides work for you on a regular basis that must be done personally by you, says when and where it is to be done, supplies the tools or other equipment and pays tax and National Insurance on your behalf, you are almost certainly an employee.

If you decide when you will work, make your own sickness and holiday arrangements (sending someone else when you can't do the work yourself) and pay your own tax and National Insurance, you are probably a self-employed person contracted to provide a service to the employer. This means that you are a worker, not an employee. To introduce some more legal jargon, the relationship you have with your employer is a 'contract for services' rather than a 'contract of employment'.

Sometimes your employer will pay your tax and National Insurance but only ask you to come to work when work is available, for example on a seasonal basis. In this situation, it is likely that you are a 'casual' worker.

It may be that you are given a contract of employment stating that you will be required to come in only when work is available. This sort of contract is commonly called a zero-hours contract. In this situation, you are an employee, but with no right to work (or pay, except for when you work). There is more on zero-hours contracts in Chapter 1.

Most people will clearly fit into one of these categories, but if you do not and fall between them then it might not be possible to say definitively which you are without a court or tribunal case. This is clearly a major problem, as many statutory rights, for example the right to redundancy pay, apply only to employees.

Some unscrupulous employers deliberately try to prevent the people who work for them becoming employees so that they do not enjoy proper employment protection. This is known as bogus self-employment.

A further confusion is that HM Revenue & Customs uses its own stricter definitions to guard against bogus self-employment being used as a tax dodge. It is perfectly possible to be taxed as an employee, but to be legally self-employed. You therefore cannot use your tax status as a guide to your employment status. There is an obvious degree of unfairness here. The law allows an employer to get away with denying you employment rights, but still makes sure that you do not get the more favourable tax treatment enjoyed by the self-employed.

Take, for example, someone who works as a cleaner in private households, working every Monday for one family, every Tuesday for another and so on. If you are in this position it is possible to be either self-employed or an employee of each family for whom you work. If you are paid by the hour, work set hours and use only cleaning tools provided by each family, you are probably employed. If the working arrangement is more flexible, you may very well be self-employed. Say you clean the house and go when you've finished, with some choice about when you do it, with no set hours, use your own tools and are free to send a friend instead. It is pretty clear here that you are being paid to perform a service, rather than being given a job. You are still a worker, but you are not an employee.

So if you are an employee you have a 'contract of employment' with your employer. Normally this will be written down, but if it is not the courts will still consider that a contract exists between you and your employer. If necessary they will rule on your contractual rights by looking at what your employer may have said to you, what has actually happened since your employment began and anything else that can help them establish the contractual relationship between you and your employer.

If you are an employee you will also enjoy the statutory rights described throughout this book, although many start only after you have worked for your employer for a qualifying period – for example, if you started a job tomorrow it would be two years until you qualified for protection against unfair dismissal.

If you are a worker, but not an employee, you do not have a contract of employment. It is likely that instead you have a 'contract for services'. You still enjoy some statutory rights, for example the minimum wage, but you will miss out on many others. There is more about your contract in Chapter 1.

Chapter One
Starting a job

The law starts to protect you as soon as you apply for a job. When you start work you gain more protection, and other rights kick in the longer you work for your employer.

Applying for and getting a job

You have some rights as soon as you apply for a job. When drawing up a shortlist or appointing the successful candidate, your employer must not discriminate against you because of sex, race, age, sexuality, marital or civil partnership status, gender reassignment, religion or belief, or disability. Nor can an employer rule you out because you are a member of a trade union or have a record of activity as a trade union member.

At some stage during the appointments process, your prospective employer is likely to ask for a reference. This is normally a statement from your previous employer or from your school or college saying that in their opinion you would be able to do the job. Your previous employer can legally refuse to give a reference, but if a reference is provided and it turns out to be inaccurate it could, in some circumstances, prevent you from getting a job or provide your employer with grounds to dismiss you. There have also been cases where employers have challenged reference providers and accused them of giving an over-favourable reference in order to get rid of someone. Nowadays it is more common for employers to provide a standard, factual reference confirming your dates of employment and job title.

Most application forms are clear that if you are found to have lied when filling in the form you will be liable to dismissal. In the past, few employers bothered to check the facts on an application form, but companies now exist that will check CVs and application forms for dishonesty, such as 'exaggerating' educational qualifications. This must be done with your agreement, but in reality there is not much of a choice, as you will be very unlikely to be considered for the job if you refuse. Honesty is, therefore, the best policy, but there are many ways of presenting your achievements in the best possible light, and many books will provide tips.

As well as asking whether they can check your references with an agency, an employer may ask you to take a drugs test. Again you can refuse, but an employer can make that refusal the grounds for not giving you the job. This would only be a problem if they were treating different applicants in different ways based on one of the unlawful forms of discrimination. If, for example, only black applicants with dreadlocks were being asked to take a drugs test, this would be unlawful racial discrimination.

Under the Immigration and Asylum Act 1996 your employer must ask you for your National Insurance number or some other evidence that you have a legal right to work in the UK. Employers must make this check for all new employees. If they limited it to one racial group or chose people they thought had foreign-sounding names they would be guilty of racial discrimination.

Employers may also ask you about criminal convictions, but you do not have to reveal them if they are 'spent'. This means the convictions happened long enough ago for the Rehabilitation of Offenders Act 1974 to allow you to keep them secret. For more information contact the National Association for the Care and Resettlement of Offenders (NACRO), whose contact details are included in Chapter 9.

If you want to work with children or vulnerable adults you will need to have a basic disclosure certificate from the Disclosure and Barring Service (DBS). This has replaced the check formerly done by the CRB. The check is requested initially by your intended employer, who will get a form from the DBS for you to fill out, but the certificate will be sent to you. Search for 'DBS' on the **www.gov.uk** website for more information.

When you accept a job offer

As soon as you have been offered a job and have accepted it, there is a basic legal contract between you and the employer, even if you have received nothing in writing. This works two ways. Firstly, it means that your employer has promised you a job. If the offer is then withdrawn it may be possible to sue your prospective employer, particularly if you have suffered loss because you have left your previous job. Breaking a contract is known as a breach of contract in legal jargon. If a court decides that your contract has been breached, it can order your employer to pay you 'damages', eg for lost wages. Secondly, it means that you have accepted the terms that are offered.

Contractual rights

The law requires your new employer to give you a written 'statement of particulars' of your employment. You should receive this within two months of starting the job. You might also be asked to sign a document called 'a contract of employment', but if not that's fine so long as you receive a written statement of particulars confirming your hours of work, location and pay details. Instead of a contract of employment you might be given a copy of a staff handbook or another document with a similar title. It's not unusual for some sections of a staff handbook to be included as part of your contract of employment. These sections will be legally binding. Information in other sections may just be provided for your information. For example, the holiday arrangements are likely to be part of your contract of employment but the location of coffee machines in your workplace will probably not.

Nothing set out in your contract can remove or reduce your statutory rights. Even if you sign a contract in which you agree to work for less than the minimum wage or if you sign away your rights to claim unfair dismissal, you are still protected. If a case went to court, any clause that denied or reduced your legal rights would be struck out as 'void'.

In the Introduction we looked at the difference between implied terms (those assumed by the court to be in any contract of employment) and express terms (those written down). But there are other ways you can gain contractual rights. If you work for an employer who recognizes a trade union and negotiates with the union about the terms and conditions enjoyed by you or people doing your job (known as 'collective bargaining'), your contract can be changed as a result of an employer–union agreement. These changes apply whether or not you are a member of the union as long as the recognition agreement covers workers on your grade or doing your job. Normally, any change to a contract agreed as a result of union negotiations will be an improvement, but there will often be a trade-off involved – more time off and better pay for agreeing to work more flexible hours, for example.

Another way you can gain contractual rights is through what is called 'custom and practice'. This means that if your employer has done something for a long time – for example, laundering staff uniforms – you might have a reasonable expectation that this should continue and, if it were to stop, that you should be notified in advance.

All contracts work two ways; while a contract sets out your employer's duties and obligations towards you, it also includes your obligations and responsibilities towards your employer. It may 'restrain' what you can do. For example, it might say that you cannot work for a rival company for six months after leaving your current job. There may be confidentiality clauses that leave you open to legal action if you pass on sensitive information to others, although the law provides protection for whistle-blowers (see pages 31–32), so if you tell commercial secrets to a rival you could end up in court, but if you tell a watchdog about a pollution cover-up you will be safe as long as you have followed the right procedures.

Frustration

Alan Warner, a site manager, had a stroke. His employer sent him his P45 with a letter confirming his employment was at an end. He lodged tribunal claims and, while the tribunal said that his employer ought to have taken steps to ascertain his medical condition and discuss the matter with him, it rejected his claims for unfair dismissal and breach of contract, finding that his contract of employment had been 'frustrated' by operation of law. See *Warner v Armfield Retail & Leisure Ltd* 2012. 'Frustration' is a somewhat obscure legal term, but can crop up in contract of employment cases. Frustration occurs when some 'reasonably unforeseeable event' takes place that makes the contract impossible or unlawful to perform, or radically different from what the parties originally intended. It means that the contract is no longer in operation. And, as there is now no contract of employment, there is no job from which you can be dismissed.

Because frustration means that there is no possibility of unfair dismissal, employers have sometimes found it an attractive argument to use in tribunal cases. Tribunals have recognized that a finding of frustration of contract removes the right to claim unfair dismissal, and have therefore tended to impose a high onus of proof on employers who claim a contract of employment has been frustrated. The matters a tribunal would take into account in deciding that a contract has been frustrated include:

- length of previous employment;

- expected future duration of employment;

- nature of the job;

- employer's need for the job to be done and the need for a replacement to do it;

- the risk to the employer of acquiring employment protection obligations towards a replacement employee;

- whether an employee has continued to be paid;

- the acts and statements of the employer in relation to the employment (in other words, is there any evidence that the employer has acted as if the contract is still in existence?);

- whether a reasonable employer could be expected to wait any longer for the employee to return.

It is important to note that there is no set time after which a contract is frustrated, and contracts have been found to have run for nearly two years even though the employee had not done any work.

Your contract may also set out benefits other than your pay, such as details of your pension or company car. It may describe your grading system and provide information on increments, performance review, performance-related pay and promotion. In general, if you work for a large company you are likely to get a detailed written contract of employment that will cover most of the issues likely to arise between an employer and employee. If you work for a smaller company, you may have a much shorter, more limited contract, but that doesn't mean you can be treated unfairly.

Both you and your employer are legally bound by the terms of your contract and by statutory laws. If you think your employer has broken the terms of your contract or broken a statutory law, you may be able to pursue a claim. There is a section on dealing with disputes about your contract in Chapter 5.

If you break the terms of your contract, this may be treated as a disciplinary matter by your employer or, in extreme circumstances, could allow them to sue you, almost certainly after dismissing you as well. Of course, if you have already left your job a court case is the only option open to your former employer.

Normally your employer cannot make changes to the terms of your contract without your agreement, although for some changes, such as an increase in salary, your employer will assume that you do not object to the change. Contracts can be written in a way that allows your employer to change your terms and conditions, usually on giving you reasonable notice. For example, your contract may state that the employer 'reserves the right to change your shift pattern in line with the needs of the business'. If you usually work the day shift and your employer needs you to work the night shift, they should give you a reasonable period of notice (in writing) of the change from days to nights. If you are unable to work the night shift, for example because of caring responsibilities, you should tell your employer as soon as possible.

If the contract does not allow your employer to change contract terms and the changes are imposed against your wishes, and you do not, in practice, accept them, your employer is likely to be in breach of contract. In other words, if the change imposed is fundamental to the contract – such as demoting you or cutting your wages – you will be able to sue your employer, either in an employment tribunal or in the civil courts depending on whether you still work for that employer. If the court finds in your favour it can order your employer to restore the original terms of your contract (and pay damages for any loss you have suffered). But you are unlikely to succeed if the change is minor (see Chapter 5 for more on this).

Zero-hours contracts

A zero-hours contract is one where the employer is not obliged to provide work for you and, if work is offered, you are not obliged to accept it. In other words, zero-hours contracts offer no assurance of hours, financial stability or job security. It is often argued that this type of working arrangement benefits certain types of worker, eg students who can 'fit work in around their studies', but it lacks the security of employment and stability of income sought after by the majority of workers. Zero-hours contracts can be particularly difficult for workers who have young children or teenagers as, without any guarantee of work, they can't plan for the future or budget effectively. Also, in workplaces where a lot of workers are on zero-hours contracts there may not be enough hours available for you and you could end up struggling to pay the bills.

Until recently, clauses written into zero-hours contracts could prevent you from working for another employer. However, the law has changed so as to ban these 'exclusivity' clauses, which means that you are now free to work for more than one employer at the same time.

If you have a zero-hours contract you will be a 'worker', which means you are entitled to rest breaks, annual holiday and sick pay and, importantly, to be paid the national minimum wage (or national living wage). You are unlikely to have 'employee' status, which carries further rights such as the entitlement to claim for unfair dismissal, to maternity pay and leave, to ask for flexible working, to statutory minimum notice periods and to redundancy payments.

Your 'written statement of employment particulars'

No later than two months after you have started your new job, you are entitled to a 'written statement of employment particulars'. This is a statement setting out your basic employment conditions. The written statement must include:

- your name and the name of your employer;
- the date when your employment started;
- your rate of pay (which must be at least at the rate of the national minimum wage), when you will be paid and how your pay has been calculated;
- your hours of work and your holiday entitlement, including public holidays (both of these must provide the maximum/minimum given under the Working Time Regulations);
- the title or description of your job and your place of work (this can state that you may be required to work in different locations);

- your notice period;
- the employer's grievance and disciplinary procedures (see pages 139–48).

You must also be informed in the statement whether your employment is permanent or for a fixed term. A fixed-term contract will specify when your employment will end, but your employer must still give you the required notice before your leaving date.

If you are employed on a fixed-term contract your employer mustn't treat you worse than an equivalent permanent employee is, or would be, treated. Nor can they keep on renewing your fixed-term contract indefinitely; after four years of continuous service you will automatically be considered permanent unless your employer can show a good reason why you should not be.

You should also be given details of any agreement with a union affecting your terms and conditions (see above) and details of any requirement to work outside the UK. The statement can refer to other documents that you may have been given, eg a staff handbook that includes information about things such as your pension.

If you have already been given a contract of employment that covers everything that is required to be in your written statement, it will count as your written statement. Strictly speaking, your written statement is not a contract of employment but it can be used as evidence of your pay and conditions in any legal proceedings or for social security purposes.

You are also entitled to a written statement about your pay with, or before, your first wage payment, whether you are paid by cash, cheque or directly into a bank account. This is known as an 'itemized pay statement'.

Other rights at work

There are many other rights at work. Some start on your first day of employment, others only after you have been in your job some time. The rest of this chapter lists the most important ones. Some only apply in practice to a small number of people or deal with very specific situations. We will mention many of them here, but you will need to go elsewhere for more detailed advice. Rights that everyone at work needs to know about are listed here and dealt with in more detail in later chapters. The chapter concludes with a list of rights and how long you have to wait before you are entitled to them.

Time off for public and workforce duties

All employees are entitled to reasonable unpaid time off to perform various public duties, including serving as a magistrate or a local authority councillor. Your contract of employment may give you a right to paid time off for such duties. Trade union representatives (where unions are recognized), union learning representatives, company pension fund trustees and designated health and safety representatives are also entitled to paid time off work to fulfil their duties.

Losing or leaving your job

Both you and your employer are entitled to a minimum period of notice of termination of employment. After one month's employment, you must give your employer at least one week's notice. Your employer must give you at least one week's notice for every year you have worked for them up to a maximum of 12 weeks, unless you are guilty of gross misconduct (for more about this see Chapter 5).

Once you have had your job for at least two years, you can ask for a written statement of reasons for your dismissal. You should be given one automatically if you get the sack while you are pregnant or on maternity leave, even if you have only just started your job. Currently you are protected against unfair dismissal only in some special circumstances as soon as you have started a job (see Chapter 7). The qualifying period for protection against unfair dismissal is two years for employees who started with their employer on or after 6 April 2012 or one year for those who started prior to that.

Public and bank holidays

Contrary to popular belief, you have no statutory right to be off work on public or bank holidays. Your contract may give you that right. If it does and you are required to work on a public holiday, you may have something else in your contract that allows for extra pay or time off in lieu of work done on bank or public holidays. Your employer is also allowed to count time off taken on public or bank holidays as part of your holiday entitlement, provided that your total annual leave entitlement does not fall below the minimum of 5.6 weeks. In other words, an employee working full-time hours is entitled to 5.6 weeks' (or 28 days') leave per year, including bank or public holidays. These changes to annual leave entitlement were implemented following a long union campaign to crack down on employers who were counting bank holidays such as Christmas Day against the four-week annual leave entitlement in European law.

Transfer of a business

If your company is taken over by another one, or if you work for a public authority and your job is transferred to a private company (or vice versa), or if your employer's contract to provide services to a client is lost to another contractor, your terms and conditions of employment may automatically transfer to the new employer. In other words, whatever is provided for in your contract with your existing employer will be 'preserved' and will pass to your new employer with no break in your continuity of employment. So, for example, you do not have to work another two years with the new employer before you can claim unfair dismissal.

You have the right to object to your contract being transferred to another employer but you should think carefully before objecting because you will be treated as having resigned. You could not claim unfair dismissal or a redundancy payment. If you transfer to the new employer before raising any objections, a tribunal is likely to say that you have accepted the new contract. However, if you do not object at the time of transfer but walk out once you have started because there has been a substantial change for the worse in your working conditions, you may have the right to claim unfair (constructive) dismissal (see Chapter 7). Walking out is always risky, and you should take advice before doing this.

If you are dismissed by either the original or the new employer, simply because of the transfer of the business or contract, the dismissal is likely to be automatically unfair and you could claim unfair dismissal in an employment tribunal. If, as is often unfortunately the case, takeovers and transfers lead to job losses for legitimate business reasons, your employer must follow the procedures for redundancy in Chapter 7.

'Transfer of undertakings', as this area of employment law is known, is particularly complex. If you have a problem in this area, you should seek legal advice. A union or advice agency will be able to help.

Sunday working

Special protection is available for some groups who may be affected by Sunday working. Shop workers who started work with their employer before 26 August 1994 and people who work in betting – either at racetracks or in licensed betting offices – who started work with their employer before 2 January 1995 can resist employer pressure to start working on Sundays.

All shop or betting shop workers can opt out of Sunday working, even if their contract of employment says they will work on Sundays, by giving three months' notice. If you choose to opt out, your employer cannot dismiss you, single you out for redundancy or punish you in any way for refusing to work on Sundays. You can get more information on this from your union or from **www.gov.uk** (see addresses section in Chapter 9).

You only have special protection, however, if you work in one of these occupations. For everyone else, Sunday is just another day of the week. In many jobs overtime payments or premiums are available for working on Sundays, but there is no legal right to them, although they may be part of your contract of employment.

Time to train

If you want to take up training opportunities during working hours you have the right to request the time to do this. You must have been an employee with the organization for a minimum of 26 weeks, and the organization must employ 250 people or more. Employers commonly pay for the training time and for courses, but they are not obliged to do so. You can only ask for training that is relevant to the job, workplace or business.

Other learning opportunities, for example to increase skills or learn new ones as part of your personal development, are often included as part of a wider workplace agreement between an employer and their workers.

Guarantee payments

If you are laid off for some reason – in other words, if there is no work for you on a particular day and you are sent home – your employer is likely to be in breach of your contract, unless the contract itself allows the employer to 'lay off', for example when demand drops or during the 'off' season. If you are laid off in these circumstances, you are entitled to a 'guarantee payment' for up to five days in any three-month period. To be entitled to a guarantee payment, you must have worked for your employer for at least one month continuously (including part-time work), you must not have refused unreasonably to do other work offered by your employer, and the lay-off must not be because of a strike.

You do not have to be paid your contractual pay, unless your contract says that you will receive full pay if you are laid off, but you must be paid the statutory minimum, which is currently the number of hours your employment contract shows you would have worked that day multiplied by the guarantee payments hourly rate, up to a limit of £26.00 per day. If there is union recognition at your workplace, better rates may well have been negotiated. The legal minimum is normally uprated in line with inflation each year, so may be a little more by the time you read this.

Insolvency of your employer

If your employer goes bust and cannot pay your wages, the Insolvency Service (0300 678 0015) will make up at least some of your lost pay. You can claim up to a maximum of £475 a week in lost wages for up to eight weeks. A maximum week's wages is normally uprated in line with inflation each year. As well as your basic wages you can claim up to six weeks' holiday pay, any company pension and up to 12 weeks' notice pay due to you. You must apply to what is known as the employer's representative, usually the liquidator, administrator or receiver. He or she will give you a form (RP1) that you must complete and send to the address shown on the form. You will then receive payment from the Insolvency Service.

Suspension on medical grounds

Your employer may suspend you from work for health and safety reasons when you are ill. This may be because your employer thinks you are likely to do damage to yourself or your fellow employees if you work. If this happens, you are entitled to up to 26 weeks' pay as long as you have worked for your employer continuously for one month and you make the claim within three months of the suspension starting. You must not refuse a reasonable offer of alternative work. The grounds for claiming medical suspension are strictly applied, so you should get advice if you think you're entitled. If your employer is not paying you, or you think they are not paying you the right amount, you may be able to make a claim to an employment tribunal.

Agency workers

All agency workers have some basic protection under the 1973 Employment Agencies Act. Laws introduced on 1 October 2011 increase protection for agency workers.

Your rights as an agency worker are based on those of someone doing a comparable (similar) job, so if there are no comparable workers or employees in the workplace you will not be entitled to treatment equal to theirs regardless of how long you work for the employer that hires you ('the hirer'). A comparable employee is someone doing the same job or broadly similar work to you usually at the same workplace, although he or she may be located elsewhere. This entitlement applies if you are working part-time as well as full-time.

From the first day of your assignment, you are entitled to access to shared facilities and amenities, such as canteen or crèche facilities, a prayer or staff room, and transport or other services provided by the hirer. You are also entitled to information on job vacancies with the hirer.

After 12 weeks on the same assignment with the same hirer you are entitled to equal treatment in relation to elements of your pay, holidays, work you do at night, rest periods and breaks, and working time. However, there is an exception to the pay part of equal treatment if you have a permanent contract of employment with a temporary work agency before undertaking work on your first assignment, which may mean that pay will be dealt with under a separate provision. However, this will include an obligation on the temporary work agency to take reasonable steps to seek suitable work for the agency worker, to provide suitable work as available and to pay minimum remuneration, even when the agency worker is not working. Equal treatment in relation to holidays, rest periods, night work and working time remains the same subject to 12 weeks' continuous employment.

If your job with the same hirer changes a lot within the 12-week period, it could mean that the role is very different now from what it was 12 weeks ago – so the qualifying period would start over again. It isn't enough that only your line manager has changed or you have moved from one site to another – there has to be a genuine and real change to the role. For instance, a combination of the following would be needed before the role could be said to have 'substantively' changed: the role requires different skills; the pay rate is different; the work is in a different location; there is a different line manager; there are different hours of work; different equipment is used; you needed to be trained for the role.

The qualifying period starts again if you move to a different assignment with a new hirer. If you work for more than one hirer you are entitled to equal treatment after 12 weeks with each hirer.

Certain breaks, for example for illness or jury service, will not send the qualifying period back to zero. Instead, the qualifying period is 'paused' and resumes once you return to work.

Pregnancy, childbirth and maternity breaks during an assignment all count towards the qualifying period, as do breaks to allow you to take adoption and paternity leave. Shared parental leave can only be taken by employees, so if you are an agency worker you will not qualify for shared parental leave, although you may be entitled to Statutory Shared Parental Pay.

If you are an agency worker:

- you are covered by health and safety law, where the agency has a responsibility not to place you in a job for which you are not appropriately qualified and the hiring company is generally responsible for providing a healthy and safe working environment for you (see Chapter 5);

- you are covered by discrimination law, which covers both the agency and the hiring company (see Chapter 6);

- you are entitled to be paid the minimum wage (see Chapter 2);

- you are entitled not to work more than an average of 48 hours a week, unless you sign an agreement with the agency saying that you are willing to work longer hours (see Chapter 3);

- you should receive 28 days' paid annual leave once you have worked for 13 weeks.

Some agencies have been getting round this by saying that your pay includes holiday pay and that they therefore do not have to pay extra if you take a break, but a European Court ruling makes clear that this is not allowed (with only some minor exceptions, mainly to deal with transitional arrangements for people paid this way in the past). It is worth checking whether your agency unambiguously offers you your legal entitlements to holiday rights and pay.

As an agency worker you may also be entitled to Statutory Maternity Pay and Statutory Sick Pay, depending on your earnings and how long you have worked for the agency. You are allowed to join a union, and a few agencies encourage their workers to do so.

If you are working as an agency worker and the hiring company offers you a permanent job, you are likely to be expected to work out a period of notice in the job as an agency temp before becoming a permanent employee of the company. Alternatively, the company may have to pay the agency a sum in lieu of notice. Any such arrangements have to be explained to you when you sign on with the agency.

There are other basic protections for agency workers:

- You have the right to be paid by your agency, on the agreed day, even if the hiring company has not paid the agency.

- You must be consulted before any changes are made to your contract or the terms under which you work.

Different rules apply in the entertainment industry. For example, it is legal to charge you a fee for trying to find you a job. If you are a musician or performer, or work in some other capacity in the entertainment business through an agency – for example, as a camera operator – you should check what the rules are (see Chapter 9 for useful addresses). The entertainment industry is well unionized, and the unions in this sector can give detailed advice to their members.

Trade union rights

Everyone in the UK has the right to join a trade union. Joining a trade union is a private matter, and you do not have to tell your employer that you have joined. On the other hand, you do not have to join a trade union, and you have legal protection in the unlikely event that you are discriminated against for not joining one.

You are free to join any union, or unions, you choose. However, it makes sense to join a trade union that is already active in your workplace. If it has recognition rights with your employer it will be in a strong position to look after you at work, accompany you if you have to go to a disciplinary hearing and so on. You will also have a say in any negotiations between the union and your employer.

But even if there is no union recognized a union can still offer help, advice and representation. Even if your employer says that they do not like unions and do not want you to join one, you can join without them finding out. Even if your employer finds out, they must not treat you differently as a result. It is unlawful for an employer to discriminate on grounds of trade union membership or activity.

If there is a collective agreement with a union in your workplace, you may be entitled to time off for attending meetings organized by the union. You would also get time off for union duties if you volunteered to become a union representative in your workplace. For details about how to join a union, see Chapter 9.

You are also protected against unfair dismissal for going on strike, as long as the strike is a legal one (the union has held a ballot and met other legal conditions before calling you out) and 'official' (the union has authorized the strike action). You are protected for the first 12 weeks of the strike.

'Whistle-blowing'

Whistle-blowing occurs when an individual reports to the authorities something seriously wrong or unlawful taking place in the organization for which he or she works. The Public Interest Disclosure Act 1998 provides rights and protection for staff who raise genuine concerns over a range of misconduct and malpractice issues. These rights cover virtually all workers, including those employed on 'worker' contracts or as contractors, trainees, agency staff or home workers, and all health professionals. However, they do not cover volunteers, the armed forces or police officers.

A worker who 'blows the whistle' will be protected if the disclosure both is made in good faith and concerns illegal activities, including crimes, theft or fraud, or actions that endanger staff, customers or the local community. In particular, the Act extends protection to all individuals who raise genuine concerns about health, safety or environmental risks.

The law expects you to use the procedures at your workplace before you take the problem to an outside body, except in the most serious cases. You can do this by using your workplace grievance procedure or by going to a senior manager or a manager other than your own. If there is a union in your workplace, talk to your union representative first. If raising the issue at work fails to resolve the situation, you can go to the appropriate official body, for example the Health and Safety Executive, the Serious Fraud Office, HM Revenue & Customs or the Audit Commission. If you work for a quango or in the NHS, it may be possible to raise the issue with the relevant government minister, but you should get advice first.

Only in very exceptional cases should an individual make wider disclosures, for example to MPs or the police. You will get protection in such cases only if the issue at stake is exceptionally serious – for example, a person's life is at risk – and you believe that the situation was not dealt with properly when you raised it internally or with the appropriate agency. You should definitely consider getting advice from your union or a legal adviser before doing so. Public Concern at Work can offer practical help and advice on whistle-blowing issues. Contact details are given in Chapter 9.

If you are dismissed or victimized after raising concerns internally, you can take a claim for reinstatement or compensation to an employment tribunal. There is no qualifying period for bringing such a claim, and compensation awards are unlimited, although they will in practice be based on your pay, how long you have worked with your employer, your future employment prospects and so on. Confidentiality clauses, such as gagging clauses in your employment contract, that conflict with the Act will not be legally binding. It is important to note, however, that you will not normally be protected for whistle-blowing to the media. In that situation you will also be at risk of a slander or libel action being brought against you by your employer. This will effectively gag you, even if you are right, and involve you in legal proceedings with costs, although reputable journalists will endeavour to protect their sources.

The Data Protection Act

Privacy at work is becoming more of an issue every day. New technology allows employers to collect substantial information about their staff, while surveillance techniques in the workplace are becoming ever more sophisticated and intrusive. Snooping is now fairly easy.

The Data Protection Act 1998 provides some important rights which individuals should be aware of, as they give employees some control over the information their employer holds on them. The Act gives all workers the right to be told about the type of information their employer holds, how that information is to be used, and anyone else with access to it. Your employer must make sure that your information is kept confidential. Only those with a legitimate reason to see information about you can do so, unless you have given your permission. Employers are not allowed to maintain 'sensitive' information on you, such as information about your sexuality, race, political or religious opinions or beliefs, union membership, health and criminal offences (except those under the Children Act 1989) in most cases, without first obtaining your permission. Employers can hold or use sensitive information where, for example, the law requires it, such as when dealing with Statutory Sick Pay.

You have the right to ask to see a copy of the information held about you by making a written request to your employer. The Data Protection Act covers personal information kept in both electronic and paper files. You can usually expect to see personnel files, information about worker movements and timesheets, appraisal forms, and papers prepared before disciplinary procedures. Film recordings and other monitoring records are also covered in some cases. The law allows you to see your references from previous employers, but not a reference provided by your current employer for a prospective employer. You can even ask to see the notes taken during job interviews. An employer must respond promptly to any written request to see information and can require a worker to pay a fee (up to £10) for producing copies. An employer can refuse to disclose information if releasing it would mean disclosing information about someone else in breach of a duty of confidence to that person or where disclosure would involve a disproportionate effort. If your employer will not tell you what information they are keeping on you, or passes your information on to someone else without your permission, you may make a complaint to the Information Commissioner's Office (see Chapter 9 for contact details).

Monitoring at work

Monitoring is to some extent a routine part of the employer–employee relationship. Most employers make some checks on the quantity and quality of work produced by their staff, and employees will generally expect and accept this.

Some employers carry out monitoring to safeguard workers, as well as to protect their own interests or those of their customers. For example, monitoring may help ensure that workers in hazardous jobs are not at risk from unsafe working practices; in some financial services employers have legal or regulatory obligations that they can only fulfil through monitoring; some employees may be at risk of attack by members of the public.

However, where monitoring goes beyond watching the performance of an individual and involves the collection, processing and storage of personal information, it needs to be done in a way that is both lawful and fair. If used in inappropriate ways or in the wrong situations, monitoring can have a negative effect on staff, intrude into their private lives, disrupt their work and interfere with the proper relationship of mutual trust and confidence between employee and employer.

The Information Commissioner has set out guidance for employers in the Employment Practices Data Protection Code. Although following the code is not a legal obligation in itself, if your employer is not adhering to it they may be breaking one or more of the laws on which it is based. For more information on the code of practice and a helpful guide for employers, you can visit the website of the government Information Commissioner at **www.ico.org.uk**.

The Data Protection Act says that workplace monitoring must be justified by the benefits that the employer and others gain from it. Therefore, the code of practice suggests that in all but the most minor cases employers carry out an 'impact assessment' when deciding if and how to use monitoring. They must also consider whether monitoring is a proportionate way of addressing a situation.

An impact assessment should:

- clearly identify the reason for the monitoring arrangement and the benefits it is likely to deliver;
- identify any likely negative effect of the monitoring on staff, including their private lives within the workplace;
- consider alternatives to monitoring, or different ways in which it might be carried out with less disruption;
- take into account the obligations that arise from monitoring;
- take into account the results of any consultation with unions or other staff representatives.

Knowledge and consent

Under the Data Protection Act, if monitoring involves the collection or other processing of personal information you should be made aware that it is being carried out and told why. Simply telling you that, for example, your e-mails may be monitored is not sufficient. You should be left with a clear understanding of when information about you is likely to be obtained, why it is being obtained and how it will be used.

Employers who have carried out a properly conducted impact assessment do not generally need the consent of individual workers to start monitoring. Consent is only likely to be an issue if your employer wants to collect sensitive information, for instance about your sexuality, race or political opinions, and there are strict rules about this (see the section on the Data Protection Act above).

The Data Protection Act restricts the ability of employers to use covert audio or video monitoring in areas that workers would genuinely and reasonably expect to be private, such as toilets, changing rooms or private offices.

Where video or audio monitoring takes place, staff should be told about the location of cameras or microphones. This information should be available in staff handbooks, on intranets or in other places where staff usually find out about personnel matters. Staff should also be told when significant changes are introduced. Where communications such as e-mails and phone calls are monitored, the information may be less specific, but staff should know when to expect that information about them will be collected.

The only exception to the principle of telling staff about monitoring is where an employer is justified in using covert monitoring to investigate a genuine suspicion of criminal activity or serious wrongdoing. If your employer is using this justification, they should have a clear intention to involve the police in the matter.

Covert monitoring

Covert monitoring means monitoring deliberately carried out in secret, so that the staff being monitored are unaware of it. It is hard for an employer to justify, and should be used only in very limited circumstances. Your employer must have genuine suspicions that criminal activity or malpractice is taking place, and that notifying individuals about the monitoring would jeopardize the employer's ability to prevent or detect the activity.

Covert monitoring must be strictly targeted at obtaining evidence within a set timeframe, and restricted to gathering evidence about the suspected malpractice. This means that it must not continue after the investigation is over, and that any other information collected during this time should be disregarded unless it reveals something that no employer could reasonably be expected to ignore.

The code also requires employers, before taking any action, to share with workers information that may have an adverse impact on them. Automated monitoring results can be incomplete or open to misinterpretation, and staff should be able to see – and if necessary explain or challenge – the results of monitoring.

Personal information collected through monitoring should not be used for purposes other than those for which the monitoring was introduced unless it is clearly in the individual's interest to do so or it reveals activity that no employer could reasonably be expected to ignore.

Monitoring e-mails, social media and web use

Personal use of your employer's e-mail system, or your employer's web access if you are using the internet, is a privilege of your job rather than a right. Many employers use automated systems to identify unacceptable use of the web, flagging up or preventing access to sites that are on a banned list or judged by an automatic system to be a risk.

Your employer has a duty to inform you if they are planning to systematically monitor your e-mails sent from work accounts. They may also frown on the use of personal e-mail accounts in work hours; and some will be checking on your use of social media. Make sure you've read and understood your employer's policy on social media, e-mail and web use. Talk to your workplace union representative if you have one, as he or she is likely to know of any such policy. If your employer doesn't have one, always assume the worst. Act cautiously, and ask your manager to clarify what is permitted.

We believe that employees should be allowed some personal use of the internet and social media in their own time at work, in the same way that they should have access to the phone for reasonable personal use. This is especially the case in workplaces where people regularly put in long hours. This privilege needs to be used responsibly, however, and balanced with the employer's valid interests in protecting their business's reputation.

An outline for a good policy on phone and digital communications

To satisfy data protection requirements, a company's policy for the use of these should, as a minimum:

- Set out clearly the circumstances in which employees may or may not use the employer's landlines, mobile phones and e-mail system and the internet for private communications.

- Have a clear policy on how and when social media can be used for tweets, posts and comments, whether professionally or privately.

- Specify clearly any restrictions on web use. A simple ban on 'offensive material' is unlikely to be clear enough for workers to know what is and is not allowed.

- Lay down clear rules regarding the personal use of digital communications when working from home.

- Explain the purposes of any monitoring, its extent, and the means used.

- Outline how the policy is enforced and the penalties for breaching it.

Your right to privacy

The best way to send any personal e-mails at work is to use a private e-mail account, rather than your work one, if your employer's policy allows this. Similarly you should use personal accounts for private tweets, posts and blogs using social media. Remember that no digital communication is ever totally secure. The only way to guarantee that you are safely using digital communications at work for personal purposes is to know that you are doing it within your rights for that workplace.

For example, your employer is entitled to access your inbox or voicemail while you are away from work if they believe that there will be business communications that need to be dealt with in your absence and if you have been told that this will happen. The employer should, however, take all possible steps to avoid accessing communications that clearly do not relate to the business.

Bear in mind, though, that this will not guarantee any level of privacy if the employer has another reason to check your e-mails or social media posts (for example, if the employer suspects criminal activity, or needs to check that the business is complying with legal obligations).

Vehicle monitoring

Technology increasingly allows employers to monitor vehicles used by workers off-site, such as company cars or delivery vehicles. Devices can record or transmit the location of the vehicle, the distance it has covered, or information about the user's driving habits.

Monitoring vehicle movements where the vehicle is allocated to a specific driver and information about the performance of the vehicle that can be linked to that driver is allowed but regulated by the Data Protection Act. Where private use of the vehicle is allowed, monitoring movements when used privately without the freely given consent of the user is rarely justifiable.

In some circumstances, though, employers are actually under a legal obligation to monitor use of vehicles, even when used privately, for example where a tachograph is fitted to a lorry. In this case the legal obligation takes precedence.

The Human Rights Act 1998

The Human Rights Act gives you additional protection at work, but can only be used as part of a complaint under employment or discrimination law. It also gives you general rights as a citizen. Drawn from the European Convention on Human Rights, the Human Rights Act is made up of 'absolute rights' and 'qualified rights'. Both are expressed in general terms, so it is sometimes difficult to predict precisely how the courts will interpret them. However, the likely implications of the Act in the workplace flow from its rights to privacy, association and freedom of expression. The data protection rules referred to above have had to take account of the right to privacy. For example, the interception of telephone calls for some limited reasons is generally only allowed under the Interception of Communications Regulations 2000 if potential users of the phone system have been informed that they might be intercepted. This would not stop your employer from checking what calls you had made or recording calls, for example for training purposes, but they could not listen in on them.

The right to free association underpins the right to join a trade union and take part in trade union activities. It gives you the right of freedom of expression (subject to defamation laws and the provisions of the Equality Act 2010). It also strengthens the right to a fair hearing in a court or tribunal.

Your rights timetable and how to use it

This is where we list all your most important statutory rights at work, how long you have to wait to be entitled to them (the qualifying period), how quickly you must make a formal application (the time limit) and the maximum compensation you can win (although actual awards are often much lower). These compensation limits are reviewed but not always increased each year. The list starts with those that protect you when you apply for a job and finishes with those for which you have to wait the longest.

TABLE 1.1 Your rights timetable

From when you apply for a job		
Your complaint:	I've been discriminated against on grounds of race, sex, disability, trade union membership age, gender reassignment, pregnancy and maternity, marriage or civil partnership, religion or belief and sexual orientation (subject to the exceptions).	
How quickly must I act?	Three months less one day from the date of the last act of discrimination. Remember to tell Acas first, as if you don't you will be prevented from lodging a claim.	Maximum compensation:	The tribunal can award compensation considered 'just and equitable' in the circumstances – no limit.

More information in Chapter 6.

From your first day at work		
Your complaint:	I've not been paid because my employer is insolvent or bankrupt.	
Time period:	Three months less one day from the date on which payment of wages ceased.	Maximum compensation:	Maximum of eight weeks' pay (from National Insurance Fund) up to £475 per week.

More information on page 26.

TABLE 1.1 *continued*

Your complaint:	There's been an unlawful deduction from my wages.
How quickly must I act?	Within three months less one day of the payroll date from which the deduction (or last in a series of deductions) is made. Where employment has terminated, within three months less one day of the effective date of termination.
Maximum compensation:	The tribunal can order the employer to make up the difference, backdating it to when the deduction started.

More information on page 50.

Your complaint:	I have been dismissed or discriminated against because: • I've raised a health and safety problem. • I've become pregnant. • I'm a trade union member or pension fund representative. • I've demanded to be paid the national minimum wage, insisted on my working time rights or taken other action against my employer. • I've taken reasonable time off for study or training, public duties or antenatal care. • I'm a shop worker or similar who has refused to work Sundays. • I blew the whistle on wrongdoings by my employer. • I complained about non-payment of the Working Tax Credit.

How quickly must I act?	Three months less one day from the date on which the alleged act or failure to act (or the date of the last in a series of acts) arose.
Maximum compensation:	Some of these rights have minimum compensation rates, eg for health and safety dismissals the minimum is £5,807. Some have maximum rates, and others, for example whistle-blowing, have no maximum. In some cases the tribunal can order the employer to make good, for example to pay you the minimum wage.
More information in Chapter 7.	
Your complaint:	I've not been given an itemized pay statement.
How quickly must I act?	Any time while in employment; within three months if employment terminates.
Maximum compensation:	The tribunal can order the employer to provide an itemized pay statement.
More information in Chapter 2.	
Your complaint:	I'm not being paid the minimum wage.
How quickly must I act?	Any time while in employment; within three months after leaving a job.
Maximum compensation:	The tribunal can order the employer to pay the difference between what you were paid and the minimum wage.
More information on page 56.	

TABLE 1.1 *continued*

Your complaint:	I've not been allowed to see the records I need to see to make sure I am getting the minimum wage.
How quickly must I act?	Three months less one day after the 14th day following receipt of production notice unless a later date agreed.
Maximum compensation:	The tribunal can order access and/or compensation of up to 80 times the current hourly minimum wage.
More information in Chapter 2.	
Your complaint:	I've been dismissed or treated unfairly because I've 'asserted a statutory right', ie taken a case against my employer such as claiming unlawful deduction from wages.
How quickly must I act?	Three months less one day starting with date of dismissal or detriment.
Maximum compensation:	If dismissed, basic award up to £475 per week's pay lost to a limit of £14,250 plus up to £78,335 compensatory award. If still working, the tribunal can order compensation and order the employer to stop the unfair treatment. No maximum.
More information in Chapter 7.	

Your complaint:	I've been dismissed or treated unfairly because I made complaints about health and safety, or for whistle-blowing.
How quickly must I act?	Three months less one day starting with date of dismissal or detriment.
Maximum compensation:	If dismissed, basic award up to £475 per week for lost pay, to a limit of £14,250. No maximum compensatory award.
Your complaint:	My employer has breached my contract.
How quickly must I act?	Claim to employment tribunal: three months less one day from the effective date of termination. Claim to court: within six years of the date on which the breach arose.
Maximum compensation:	Maximum in tribunals of £25,000. Limit of £50,000 in lower (county or sheriff) courts, unlimited in higher courts.

More information on page 174.

Your complaint:	I've been sacked because of a protected characteristic.
How quickly must I act?	Three months less one day starting with effective date of termination.
Maximum compensation:	No limit on compensation. Amount that tribunal considers 'just and equitable' in the circumstances.

More information in Chapter 6.

TABLE 1.1 *continued*

Your complaint:	I'm not getting the proper rest breaks set out in the working time rules.		
How quickly must I act?	Three months less one day starting on the day on which the failure (or the last in the series of failures) occurred.	*Maximum compensation:*	Unlimited and/or the tribunal can order the employer to provide proper rest breaks for you.
More information in Chapter 3.			
Your complaint:	I'm getting paid less than a man/woman doing equal work because of my sex.		
How quickly must I act?	At any time during employment or within six months less one day of the date on which the contract is terminated (even if re-engaged by the same employer).	*Maximum compensation:*	The tribunal can order the employer to provide equal pay and can order compensation backdated pay for up to six years.
More information in Chapter 6.			
One month less one day from the start of your job			
Your complaint:	I've been laid off but not paid (guarantee pay).		
How quickly must I act?	Three months less one day starting with the day for which payment claimed.	*Maximum compensation:*	£26.00 per day.
More information on page 25.			

Your complaint:	I have been suspended on medical grounds.		
How quickly must I act?	If employed for one month or longer – entitled to be paid for up to 26 weeks of suspension at rate of 'normal week's pay'. Three months less one day starting with effective date of suspension.	*Maximum compensation:*	The pay you have lost.
More information on page 26.			

Two months less one day from the start of your job

Your complaint:	I've not been given a written statement of employment particulars.		
How quickly must I act?	Any time while in employment; within three months if employment terminates.	*Maximum compensation:*	The tribunal can order the employer to provide a written statement; the amount of compensation will be between two and four weeks' pay at the tribunal's discretion.
More information on page 15.			

After 13 weeks' employment

Your complaint:	I'm not getting paid holidays.		
How quickly must I act?	Three months less one day from the date when the leave should have been permitted to begin.	*Maximum compensation:*	Unlimited and/or the tribunal can order the employer to give you your leave entitlement.
More information in Chapter 3.			

TABLE 1.1 *continued*

After two years in your job (one year if employment began on or before 6 April 2012)		
Your complaint:	I've been dismissed unfairly.	
How quickly must I act?	Three months less one day from the effective date of termination.	*Maximum compensation:* Basic award up to £475 per week's pay lost, to a limit of £14,250 plus up to £78,335 compensatory award.
More information in Chapter 7.		
Your complaint:	I've been dismissed because my employer has sold the business to another company.	
How quickly must I act?	Three months less one day starting with the effective date of termination.	*Maximum compensation:* Basic award up to £475 per week's pay lost, to a limit of £14,250 plus up to £78,335 compensatory award.
More information on page 23.		
Your complaint:	I've not been given written reasons for dismissal.	
How quickly must I act?	Three months less one day starting with effective date of termination.	*Maximum compensation:* Two to four weeks' pay at the tribunal's discretion.
More information in Chapter 7.		

Your complaint:	I've not been allowed to return to work after additional maternity leave.	
How quickly must I act?	Three months less one day after notified day of return when employer refuses right.	*Maximum compensation:*	Compensation to reflect what the tribunal considers 'just and equitable' in the circumstances.

More information on pages 93–94.

Your complaint:	I have not been allowed to take parental leave or time off for a family emergency under the terms of the regulations.	
How quickly must I act?	Three months less one day.	*Maximum compensation:*	Compensation to reflect what is 'just and equitable' in the circumstances, at the tribunal's discretion.

More information on pages 107–113.

After two years less one day

Your complaint:	I've not been paid my redundancy pay.	
How quickly must I act?	Six months less one day starting from the date of dismissal.	*Maximum compensation:*	See Chapter 7. Maximum £14,250 statutory redundancy pay.

More information on page 188.

All the figures given for compensation are correct for 2015. Most are uprated, often by inflation, on 1 February each year.

Chapter Two
Payday

It is good to have a satisfying and worthwhile job, but most of us work because we need the money as well. This chapter sets out the law about your pay – what your employer must tell you, what they can deduct from your pay and the minimum they must pay you.

Deductions from wages

Your contract of employment or 'written statement of employment particulars' will say how much you are going to be paid. It must be at least the minimum wage, described later in this chapter. If you do not receive the pay promised in your contract or written statement, your employer has made an 'unauthorized deduction from wages' and you can take a claim to an employment tribunal (see Chapter 8). This statutory right covers all workers, not just employees (see page 10 for this important distinction).

There are, however, four ways in which it is legal for your employer to take money from your wage or salary:

- Your employer can deduct income tax and National Insurance. This must be for the correct amount. If you think it is not, contact HM Revenue & Customs (HMRC) and it will repay you if the amount deducted was wrong, or investigate your employer if there is a suspicion of fraud.

- Your employer can take money if you have given permission. For example, you may agree to make a payroll contribution to a charity, to a staff social club or to a trade union. You can, however, withdraw your permission at any time.

- Your employer can make a deduction from your wage packet if your contract allows this to happen, as long as you have seen the contract with this in it before you start work, or your employer has explained in writing to you that they intend to take the money and you have agreed to it. This then becomes part of your contract.

- Your employer can deduct money at source if required to by law, eg a court order against you to make child maintenance payments.

If your employer has overpaid you the previous time you were paid, they may take that from your next pay packet without asking you. If your contract allows your employer to take money away as part of a disciplinary process, they can do this without asking you (see Chapter 5). If you take part in a strike, your employer can take money from your wages without asking you. In this situation, your union may give you strike pay.

There are some jobs that allow your employer to deduct money if there is a cash shortage owing to theft. The key test is whether you deal with the public and handle money. So if you are a shop worker or your job involves selling goods to the public you can have money deducted from your wages if there is a shortfall. This can also happen if you collect money, say as a rent collector. But it does not apply if you deal only in business-to-business transactions, perhaps as a lorry driver supplying goods to a warehouse.

Your employer cannot deduct more than 10 per cent of your cheque, salary or wage packet. They can keep on making a 10 per cent deduction until the loss is paid off. The 10 per cent is before tax or National Insurance is deducted. Depending on your tax situation, this may mean that in practice more or less than 10 per cent of your take-home pay may be deducted. However, if you are leaving your job, whether because you have resigned or retired or been dismissed, your employer can deduct any amount of your final pay packet and any notice pay (see Chapter 7) to make up the shortfall.

Your employer must start making any deductions from your wages within 12 months of the loss occurring. But while they cannot start deductions after 12 months they can continue if they have already started before the 12-month limit. A new deduction, however, would be unlawful, and you can take a tribunal case.

The law on 'unauthorized deductions' covers issues such as holiday pay, bonuses, Statutory Sick Pay (SSP) and luncheon vouchers. It does not cover expenses, loans or advances of wages, pensions or redundancy payments, tips, or payments in kind.

If you think that your employer has wrongly deducted money from your wages you should raise the matter with them first, or with the finance department if you work for a large company. It may be that a genuine mistake was made. If this is not the case, you can make a complaint to an employment tribunal (see Chapter 8) and the tribunal can order the employer to pay the money.

Sick pay rights

When they talk about their sick pay, most workers mean the scheme operated by their employers. There are no national rules for these schemes, and many exclude some people, such as new staff.

But you do have rights to Statutory Sick Pay, a flat-rate benefit, paid by your employer, in accordance with national rules. If you are covered, your employer must either pay you SSP when you qualify or open up the company scheme to you and offer you benefits that are at least as good.

This is a complicated subject, and this section has to simplify some points. If you have any problems claiming SSP, make sure you get advice and support from your union or an advice agency as soon as possible.

Qualifying for Statutory Sick Pay

You will qualify for SSP for up to 28 weeks if:

- You are an employee – see page 10 for the difference between an employee and a worker. This includes most agency workers. As long as you are an employee it does not matter whether you work part-time or have only just started work with an employer.

- You earn enough to pay National Insurance contributions (£112 a week from April 2016). If your pay fluctuates, your average earnings are calculated over a period of eight weeks before your SSP starts.

- You are incapable of carrying out your normal work for at least four consecutive days because you are sick or have a disability.

You don't have to have actually paid any National Insurance contributions.

You will *not* qualify if:

- you are self-employed;
- you have not yet started work.

Claiming Statutory Sick Pay

- You should notify your employer that you are sick, using any procedures in place for this. SSP should then automatically be paid to you if you are entitled to it, in the same way as your normal wages.

- You can get SSP for up to 28 weeks if your sickness lasts that long.

- You will not be paid for the first three days – these are called 'waiting days'.

- Two periods of sickness within 56 days are treated as linked. This means that there are no further 'waiting days' but previous periods of entitlement count towards the 28-week limit.

- You are not entitled to SSP once your contract of employment ends, nor once your Maternity Allowance (MA) or Statutory Maternity Pay (SMP) period begins. If you are on maternity leave and you are not entitled to SMP or MA, you cannot get SSP for a period of 18 weeks.

- Employers can ask for 'reasonable evidence' of incapacity. In practice, this usually means a self-certification form for the first seven days (including the waiting and other non-working days) and a doctor's certificate after that. This is now known as a 'fit note', and it will say either that you are 'not fit for work' or that you 'may be fit for work'; if it says that you may be fit for work but you and your employer agree that you should remain off work, you should still get SSP.

- If your employer dismisses you to avoid paying SSP you may have a claim for unfair dismissal at an employment tribunal. The SSP rules, in any case, require your employer to go on paying you SSP until you are no longer entitled to the benefit (or your contract comes to an end, if this is earlier).

- If there is a stoppage of work owing to a trade dispute that began *before* you became sick, you will not be entitled to SSP for the whole period of incapacity, even if the dispute ends. On the other hand, if the stoppage began *after* you became sick, you will continue to be entitled to SSP.

How much will you get?

SSP is currently paid at a flat rate of £88.45 a week. If you have two or more jobs, and earn more than enough to pay National Insurance contributions in both, you can claim SSP in each.

Sick of the sack

Joyce Khan was a night-duty nurse, but became ill and was off sick for some time. Under NHS rules (part of her contract of employment) she was entitled to sick pay of two months' full pay and two months' half-pay. But when this four-month period came to an end Joyce was sacked.

However, the booklet setting out NHS sick pay provisions said nothing about dismissal at the end of the sick pay period. Her managers said that such a rule existed nationally in the Health Service and that it had been applied to other cases. But Joyce had, in fact, already sent in a medical certificate indicating that within 10 days of her sick pay running out she expected to be back on duty. Apparently this certificate had never reached the attention of the officer who dealt with the dismissal.

She claimed unfair dismissal and won. The tribunal said that Joyce's managers had not acted reasonably. A rule that dismissal should be automatic on termination of sick pay, regardless of individual circumstances, was outmoded. Secondly, there had been bad communication between departments concerning the medical certificate, and thirdly there had been no consultation with the employee concerned before dismissal.

Tribunal cases have established what an employer should do before dismissal for sickness, and there is guidance in the Acas Code of Practice on Disciplinary and Grievance Procedures. Employers should: consult the employee and discuss the problem with him or her; take steps to enable them to take a balanced view of the problem (this will include taking steps to ascertain the medical situation); and consider whether suitable alternative work is available.

It is possible for an employer to dismiss a worker fairly for genuine sickness by reason of capability. But tribunals tend to look carefully at the reasonableness in such cases. They will consider: the length of past and future service of the employee; how vital the employee is to the employer's business and how easy it is to find a temporary replacement; and the effect of the absence on the business and other employees.

The question a tribunal will ask is whether the time has come where a reasonable employer is entitled to say enough is enough. The key is then likely to be the future sickness of the worker. But the employer must also ensure that they are not breaking the Equality Act 2010 and its provisions on disability discrimination (see Chapter 6).

The wage minimum for 25s and over

The national living wage for those aged 25 and over was introduced on 1 April 2016. It is mandatory and set at £7.20 per hour, rising to £9 an hour by 2020. It is expected that it will apply in the same way (but only for that age group) as the national minimum wage – see below.

The wage minimum for 24s and under, and apprentices

Coverage

Younger workers (aged 24 and under) and apprentices are legally entitled to the national minimum wage (NMW). You are covered whether or not you have a written contract of employment. Home workers, agency workers and piece and commission workers are all entitled to the NMW. So are workers on temporary contracts and part-time workers. However 'casual' the work, you are still entitled to be paid the NMW. Agricultural workers in Scotland and Northern Ireland are currently covered by a different set of minimum wages, depending on age and qualification, as are agricultural workers in England who were employed before 1 October 2013. An Agricultural Advisory Panel for Wales was established in 2016, which may set higher minimum wages for workers in Wales. The different agricultural worker minimum rates are available from the Pay and Work Rights Helpline: 0800 917 2368 or the Labour Relations Agency Helpline in Northern Ireland: 028 9032 1442.

The following groups are *not* entitled to the NMW:

- family workers, including those working for a family business;

- people working within a family, sharing tasks and leisure activities, for example au pairs;

- trainees on government-funded schemes such as employment programmes;

- students on work placements, including teacher-training placements;

- the armed forces;

- prisoners;

- share fishermen;

- mariners and offshore workers based entirely outside the UK;

- voluntary workers (who must work for a charity, voluntary organization, school or hospital and must not receive any payments other than reasonable expenses or benefits in kind or, in certain circumstances, subsistence payments). Some people who are considered volunteers may actually be workers who should be paid the NMW because they have what amounts to a contractual relationship. These include some internships that have not been arranged as an integral part of an educational course.

In some sectors where there are many more people who would like a job than there are vacancies, such as politics, the media and entertainment, some employers demand a period of free work variously described as a placement, work experience or other euphemism before considering someone for a paid job. This is a racket and is likely to be in breach of the NMW.

Work experience can of course be educational, and there is a fine line to be drawn here. If the experience is arranged by a school or college, there is probably no legal problem. If it is implicitly or explicitly a try-out period to see if an employer wants to give you a job, there is almost certainly a breach of the law. A good source of advice is the National Council for Work Experience.

The treatment of the self-employed can be complicated. As we saw in the Introduction it is possible to be a worker without being an employee. Both employees and workers are, however, covered by the NMW. If you have a contract for services rather than a contract of employment you are still entitled to the minimum wage. If, however, you are genuinely self-employed, effectively running your own business and cannot be said to have an employer, you are not covered by the NMW. Your tax status is once again not a guide to your minimum wage status. You can be treated as self-employed by the tax office but still be eligible for the minimum wage. If in doubt, take advice.

NMW hourly rates

You are entitled to be paid the NMW for each hour you work, but young workers are entitled to a lower rate than older workers, as are some workers receiving training. Hourly rates from 1 October 2015 are:

adult workers aged 21–24	£6.70
18- to 20-year-olds	£5.30
16- to 17-year-olds above the school leaving age	£3.87
apprentices aged up to 18 and older apprentices in the first year of their apprenticeship	£3.30
the accommodation offset	£5.35

Rates usually increase in October each year. For workers aged 25 and over see 'The wage minimum for 25s and over' above.

Calculating your hourly pay

Hourly pay for the NMW is worked out as an average over your pay period. If you are paid weekly your pay period is a week; if you are paid daily it is a day; and if you are paid monthly it is a month. Some people are paid in arrears. For example, your pay for the work you do one week may be actually paid in the next week.

Working out your hourly pay for most people is a simple matter of dividing your total pay (before tax and other deductions) by the number of hours you worked. But there can be complications, and there are rules about both what does and does not count as pay and how your hours of work are counted.

What counts as pay?

Your pay may be made up of a mix of different elements. The following *do* count towards your hourly rate:

- gross pay – before National Insurance, tax or pension deductions;
- piece rates, sales commissions and any performance-related pay;
- a bonus (though it must be allocated mainly to the pay period in which it is paid);
- tips paid through the payroll, though tips paid in cash directly to staff are in addition to your hourly rate.

The following do *not* count:

- pension, retirement or redundancy payments;
- overtime and shift payments;
- expenses or money spent on work refunded by the employer;
- allowances such as London weighting;
- loans or advances of wages;
- any benefits in kind, such as meals, luncheon vouchers, car allowance or medical insurance, except accommodation, which is dealt with below.

This means that any payments for overtime, for example, or London weighting must be in addition to an average hourly rate of at least the NMW. Your employer cannot pay you £5 an hour for an eight-hour day and then £10 an hour for an extra four hours' overtime and claim that on average you were getting more than the minimum wage. Overtime payments cannot be used to boost a basic average that is below the NMW. Nor can an employer add a notional amount to your pay to take it to the minimum wage level but then deduct it again to pay for any meals or drinks provided free.

If accommodation is provided as part of your job, your employer can deduct a maximum of £5.35 for every day accommodation is provided. This means that a maximum of £37.45 per week for accommodation can be deducted from your pay.

The accommodation charge is the only deduction that an employer can make from the minimum wage for non-pay benefits. Your employer may not charge for travel, meals, uniforms or services such as gas, water and electricity if to do so would take your pay below the minimum wage. Employers cannot charge for protective clothing or other necessary health and safety equipment in any circumstances. The law also stops employers from getting round these restrictions by splitting their business into separate employment and accommodation agencies.

What counts as working hours?

Hourly paid and salaried workers are entitled to be paid the NMW for:

- time at work and required to be at work;
- time on standby or on call at or near work;
- downtime at work caused by machine breakdown;
- time travelling to training or business appointments during normal working hours;
- training time during normal working hours.

If you are hourly paid, the NMW legislation does not give you the right to be paid for rest breaks, sick leave or maternity leave. However, under your employment contract you may be entitled to be paid for these hours too.

Output-only work

Some workers have no set hours but are paid only for the output they produce. Most home workers engaged in manufacturing or envelope-stuffing jobs are paid in this way, as are many newspaper and leaflet distributors and travelling salespeople.

If you have set hours and are paid by results, you are not an output worker but a time worker and should simply be paid the minimum wage. Employers can also choose to pay the minimum wage for each hour worked to genuine output workers as well. There are, however, some special provisions for output workers, because employers often have no way of checking how many hours such workers have actually worked.

Employers are allowed to use what is called the 'fair piece rates' system. This requires them to establish how long it takes an average worker to do the job. They should do this by timing a fair sample of workers to get an average time and then adding 20 per cent to allow for fatigue during the day.

Unmeasured work

A small number of workers undertake 'unmeasured work'. This means they have fixed tasks, but no fixed hours of work. Examples might include hostel wardens or domestic workers with no fixed hours. Workers undertaking unmeasured work either must be paid at least the NMW for every hour worked or can agree a 'daily average' agreement with their employer. This would identify the number of hours likely to be worked daily, and must be a realistic average. The worker must then be paid at least the NMW for this number of hours each day.

Your right to see your records

Employers are required to keep sufficient records to establish that they are paying workers at least the NMW and workers have the right to see and copy their records. If you want to see your records, you must ask your employer in writing. The employer must produce the records within 14 days. You have the right to be accompanied by someone of your choice when you inspect your records.

What to do if you are not receiving the NMW

Your rights

Under the NMW legislation, you have the right:

- to be paid at least NMW rates;
- to see your records (accompanied) as set out above;
- not to be dismissed or victimized as a result of attempts to be paid or ensure you are eligible for the NMW.

If you are not receiving the NMW, or have been refused access to your records or have been victimized as a result of trying to claim the NMW, you can get help to enforce your rights.

Take advice

If you are a trade union member, your union will be able to give you advice on your rights, accompany you to see your records and help you take a case to an employment tribunal if you are not receiving your rights. Other agencies, including the Citizens Advice Bureau, can also help and advise. Their numbers are given in Chapter 9.

National helpline and enforcement officers

HMRC is responsible for enforcing the NMW. The first point of contact is the official Pay and Work Rights Helpline: 0800 917 2368. Calls are confidential. The helpline gives information and advice on the NMW and passes on complaints to HMRC. Enforcement officers at HMRC can help you to take enforcement action against your employer if you are not receiving what you are entitled to.

Enforcement officers have legal powers to enable them to enforce the NMW. They can require your employer to provide information about NMW pay, and inspect your employer's premises to gain access to pay records. Enforcement officers impose a fixed penalty of up to £20,000 on employers failing to pay the NMW. They also take action to make your employer start paying back what you are owed. The enforcement officers can also help workers take their employer to an employment tribunal, or take a case on behalf of the worker in cases where employers try to resist paying up. HMRC can also pursue claims for ex-workers who have left the offending employer. This matters, because most workers actually make their complaint after they have resigned. Every year HMRC recovers around £4 million for underpaid workers.

Deliberate refusal to pay the NMW is a criminal offence. If an employer continues to refuse payment, the enforcement officer can prosecute them in the criminal courts.

Employment tribunal or civil courts

You can bring a case against your employer in an employment tribunal or in the civil courts to recover any money owed as a result of not receiving the NMW. The civil courts can be useful in cases that fall outside the strict time limits that apply to employment tribunal claims. It is up to the employer to show that they have paid you the NMW. You do not have to prove that you have not received it, though in practice you will need to be able to disprove your employer's claim.

You are, however, probably best advised to make every effort to get HMRC's enforcement officers to take up your case if possible, especially if it is a clear-cut case. Tribunals are more likely to hear test cases, where the rules are not entirely clear.

You can also take a claim to an employment tribunal for unfair dismissal or victimization if you have lost your job or suffered some other action from your employer resulting from trying to enforce your right to be paid the NMW.

The living wage

This is an hourly wage level set by the Living Wage Foundation below which it considers people would struggle to cope with the basic cost of living. Adjusted annually, the current UK living wage is £8.25 an hour and for London it is £9.40 an hour, regardless of age. These rates are currently much higher than the national living wage (see page 56) and the national minimum wage. However it has no legal force; employers choose to pay it on a voluntary basis.

Tax credits and salary sacrifice schemes

Tax credits are a way of providing extra income to parents and low-paid workers. They are notoriously complicated, and this guide does not have the space to explain all the rules – if you have more detailed questions a good place to start is the Tax Credit Helpline: 0345 300 3900 or Working Families Helpline for parents and carers: 0300 012 0312.

There are two tax credits:

- Child Tax Credit (CTC) supports families with children, regardless of whether anyone in the family has a paid job.

- Working Tax Credit (WTC) helps low-paid workers (including some workers without children) by topping up their earnings.

You claim them on the same form, and you may be entitled to one or the other, or both.

Rules that apply to both CTC and WTC

There are some general rules about who can get CTC and WTC:

- You must be at least 16 years old.
- Normally, you must live in the UK.
- You must not be subject to immigration control.
- If you are a member of a couple (married, civil partners or living with someone as if you are married or civil partners), you must claim together, as the circumstances of both will be taken into account.

Child Tax Credit

CTC helps families with children, whether or not you are in employment. To qualify, you must be responsible for at least one child or young person:

- a child (people are counted as children until 31 August after their 16th birthday); or
- a young person aged 16 to 19 and in full-time non-advanced education or unwaged, approved training; or
- a young person aged 16 or 17 who has registered for work or training with a qualifying body.

CTC is normally paid direct to the bank account of the person with main responsibility for caring for the children (if you also qualify for the childcare element of WTC, you will be paid this at the same time). CTC is made up of two parts:

- the *family element*, for every family with children (this element is being abolished from 2017);
- a *child element* for each child, paid at a higher rate for disabled children and an enhanced rate for severely disabled children.

CTC is designed to give the most support to families who need it most. A family with two children and an income of £30,000 a year qualify for some CTC, but could still qualify on a higher income, depending on their circumstances.

Working Tax Credit

WTC tops up the incomes of people with low incomes who are employed or self-employed, including some people who do not have children. It provides extra support for disabled people and helps with childcare costs.

You can qualify for WTC if:

- you are aged 25 or over and work for at least 30 hours a week;

- you are a lone parent and work at least 16 hours a week;

- you are a couple with children and one of you is incapacitated, entitled to carer's allowance, or in hospital or prison, and the other works at least 16 hours a week;

- you are a couple with children and work at least 24 hours a week (you can combine hours, but one of you must be working at least 16 hours a week);

- you are disabled and work at least 16 hours a week (you must have a disability that puts you at a disadvantage in getting a job and get a qualifying benefit, or were getting one before you started work); or

- you are aged 60 or over and work at least 16 hours a week.

WTC is normally paid direct to your bank or building society. If you and your partner both work 16 hours or more a week, you will have to choose to whom it is paid.

WTC is made up of a series of elements:

- a basic element;

- an element for lone parents and couples;

- an element for working a total of at least 30 hours a week (only one element per couple);
- a disability element;
- a severe disability element;
- a childcare element – see below.

You receive the maximum amount of WTC until you reach an 'income threshold' of £6,420. For every £1 you earn over the income threshold your WTC is reduced by 41p.

From April 2016, any increase in annual household income over £2,500 counts when calculating your entitlement for that year, whereas previously increases of up to £5,000 were ignored.

The rate of CTC and WTC (excluding disability elements) was frozen for four years from April 2016, and the 'benefit cap' – the maximum benefit a non-working household can receive – was reduced from £26,000 to £23,000 for families living in London and to £20,000 for those outside London.

Like CTC, the WTC is designed to provide the most help to the people who need it most, and the amount you will actually get depends on how high your income from other sources is. A couple without children can have an income of £18,000 a year and still qualify for some WTC, or more depending on their circumstances.

Help with childcare

WTC can also help with the costs of childcare – this is known as the 'childcare element'. To qualify, you must be:

- a lone parent employed for at least 16 hours a week; or
- a member of a couple where both partners work at least 16 hours a week; or
- a member of a couple where one partner works 16 hours a week and the other is incapacitated, entitled to carer's allowance, in hospital or in prison.

The childcare element pays for up to 70 per cent of the costs of registered or approved childcare, up to a limit of £175 a week for one child or £300 for two or more.

Your childcare element is added to the other WTC elements you qualify for, and the total amount you get will depend on your income (joint income for couples) but it will not necessarily be paid in the same way. If you qualify for the childcare element, this is always paid direct to the person with main responsibility for caring for the children, alongside the CTC, even if he or she is not the person who receives the WTC.

Salary sacrifice schemes

Many organizations now offer salary sacrifice schemes. The idea behind this is quite simple. You give up part of your salary and, in return, your employer gives you a non-cash benefit, such as childcare vouchers or increased pension contributions.

Once you accept a salary sacrifice, your overall pay is lower, so you pay less tax and National Insurance.

Sacrificing part of your salary means you earn less. This might affect maternity pay or mortgage applications. Lower earnings may also affect your state pension or contribution-based state benefits such as Jobseeker's Allowance and Employment and Support Allowance. However, you may be able to claim more tax credits.

How salary sacrifice affects tax credits

Accepting childcare vouchers from your employer may affect your tax credits. If you're already getting tax credits to help with childcare costs, you're probably better off not opting for salary sacrifice. That's because you can only claim tax credits for the childcare you pay with your own money, rather than with vouchers. To check, go to **www.gov.uk/childcare-vouchers-better-off-calculator**.

New childcare scheme

From September 2017 (and earlier in some areas) working parents of three- and four-year-olds will be able to get 30 hours' free childcare a week, worth around £5,000 a year per child.

The existing childcare voucher scheme will run until the new scheme, Tax-Free Childcare, is launched. When it starts, you can get 20 per cent of your childcare costs paid for by the government. However, low-income workers may be better off staying on tax credits or Universal Credit, and you cannot get Tax-Free Childcare at the same time.

Extra help

You can check whether you qualify for tax credits online at **www.gov.uk/qualify-tax-credits**, and the website also provides extra information about tax credits.

There is a Tax Credits Helpline, which can help you make a claim or report changes in your circumstances, open Monday to Friday 8 am to 8 pm, Saturday 8 am to 4 pm: 0345 300 3900. Textphone: 0345 300 3909. Welsh helpline: 0845 302 1489.

Chapter Three
Working time rights

Thanks to Europe's Working Time Directive, most people now have seven basic rights to proper time off, rest breaks and paid holiday:

- 5.6 weeks' paid holiday a year;
- a 20-minute rest break when the working day is more than six hours;
- a rest period of 11 hours every working day;
- a rest period of 24 hours once every seven days;
- a ceiling of 48 hours on the maximum average working week;
- a ceiling of an average of eight hours' night work in every 24;
- free health assessment for night workers.

Working time rights can be complicated, have proved controversial and are barely enforced. Employer organizations successfully lobbied the UK government for exemptions and opt-outs that do not apply in the rest of Europe. The European directive, on which UK law is based, is far from comprehensive. There are many problems of definition, such as what exactly counts as working time, and many provisions can be varied by agreement between the employer and the workforce.

People in the UK work among the longest hours in Europe, with more than 3 million working more than 48 hours per week. In some industries and sectors this is because many hours of overtime are worked. Security guards working for the minimum wage need the overtime to earn a decent income. In other sectors long hours are built into the system, with junior hospital doctors probably the best-known example.

For white-collar workers the basic problem is unpaid overtime. It is rare for employees doing these types of job to have their hours counted, as they will not normally get overtime pay, but many offices and other workplaces are still gripped by a long-hours culture. Often nothing is said directly, but the sheer volume of work, pressure from colleagues, job insecurity and wanting to get on have all conspired to keep people at work for longer and longer hours.

Many such jobs are rewarding and interesting. Work does not always come along in neat nine-to-five parcels, but it is easy for working hours to ratchet up a little more each year. Work and family life get out of balance. Stress and exhaustion levels rise. To call time on Britain's long-hours culture is not to go back to clockwatching, but to understand that other countries manage to combine better living standards, shorter working hours and more productive workplaces.

Then of course there are those who are missing out on their most basic rights to paid holidays and proper rest breaks. When the Working Time Regulations (WTR) first came into force in 1998, around 2 million people won their first-ever rights to paid holidays. Some are still missing out, or are being made to pay in other ways for their own holidays.

This chapter aims to guide you through the working time maze. It cannot provide all the answers, but it should tell you whether you are getting your working time rights, whether you are clearly missing out, or whether you are in a grey area where you will need to take detailed advice based on your own circumstances.

Exemptions from Working Time Regulations

Some groups of workers are covered by their own special rules. Others miss out on some rights but not others. If you are under 18 the rules are different, and you should make sure you read the section on pages 88–89 at the end of this chapter. The following groups are covered:

- *Transport workers:* 'Non-mobile' transport workers such as station staff have been fully covered since 2003, while 'mobile' rail staff such as drivers and guards as well as non-HGV/PSV drivers of road vehicles are partly covered. These workers are entitled to an average maximum working week of 48 hours; however, they are only entitled to 'adequate' rest, rather than the stronger rights to breaks and rest periods that apply to most workers. There is no definition of 'adequate', but the TUC believes that it needs to be as good as 'compensatory rest' (see below). Staff who work at a transport location, such as people who unload lorries or who work in shops in stations, are covered by the working time rules.

- *HGV and PSV drivers* get 5.6 weeks' paid leave. They are also covered by the rules in the Road Transport Working Time Regulations, which limit their hours to 48 a week without any opt-out. However, many employers try to misuse the loophole that allows waiting time known about in advance not to count toward the 48-hour week.

- *Seafarers* are covered by separate rules.

- *Aviation and cabin crew* have their own rules too.

- *Junior doctors in training* have been covered by the 48-hour limit since 2009.

- *Armed forces and civil protection services* (such as the police, but not all civil protection personnel) are excluded.

Ambulance personnel, fire-fighters and prison staff are covered by the regulations. You will need to take more advice if you work in this category. Most workers in civil protection outside the armed forces or the police are in a trade union. This should be your first port of call for further advice.

- *Domestic staff in a private household* are partially excluded. They are entitled to rest breaks and paid holidays, but not to the 48-hour average week or night work rights.

- *Those whose 'working time is not measured or pre-determined'* are exempt from all other working time rights – although workers in this category are entitled to paid holidays.

This last exemption has been the subject of much argument in Britain. The European directive is clear that this is meant to be a narrow exclusion aimed at relatively small groups in the work-force. These include top managers who are free to set their own hours (perhaps because they own the business or have no one to tell them what to do), workers employed by other members of their family, and some people with unusual jobs such as ministers of religion.

Employer organizations have argued that this exemption should apply to the majority of white-collar workers for work they do on a 'voluntary' basis outside the hours set down in their contract of employment, but the European Court of Justice has ruled against this broad interpretation. We explain this later in the chapter.

Happy holidays!

Your holiday rights start on the first day of your job – you do not have to build up holiday rights. Everyone at work is entitled to a minimum of 5.6 weeks' paid leave each year. The number of days you will actually receive as holiday depends on how many days a week you work. If you work full-time five days a week you should, therefore, get 5.6 lots of five days – that's 28 days – of paid leave every year (including bank and public holidays). If you work part-time you should get 5.6 times what you work on average each week. For example, if you work three days a week then you should get (5.6 × 3 =) 16.8 days' holiday.

Christmas Day and other holidays can count as part of your annual entitlement as long as you are paid for them. The European minimum is only four weeks. The UK was the only EU country that allowed public holidays to count against this minimum. A long union campaign led the government to deal with this by extending the four-week minimum by eight days for full-time workers, reaching 5.6 weeks in 2009, as there are eight bank holidays in Britain. You can also take unpaid time off if you have young children or suffer a family emergency such as looking after a sick child. This is explained in Chapter 4,

When you can take your holidays

You do not have an absolute right to choose when you take your holiday. Unless your contract says otherwise, your employer can refuse requests, rule out all holiday at particular times of the year and even direct you to take your holiday when it suits them without any consultation with you. If you are requesting a holiday, the regulations say that you must give your employer sufficient notice. This is twice the number of days of leave that will be taken – to take four days off work you must therefore give eight working days' notice.

But while you must give this notice it does not guarantee that you will get the holiday, as your employer is free to refuse leave requests. On the other hand, there is nothing to stop your employer granting requests at extremely short notice. In practice, most well-run organizations will have their own rules about deciding leave.

More importantly, the same notice period applies to your employer if they are telling you when you must take a holiday. They cannot therefore force you to take a fortnight's leave because an order is suddenly cancelled. They must give you four weeks' notice – twice the period of the leave – if they are to make you take two weeks off.

Your employer must also give you notice if they want to rule out some periods when staff cannot take leave. The period of notice must be the same as the period during which holiday cannot be taken. In other words, if the employer wants to stop people taking holidays for the four-week period before Christmas, four weeks' notice must be given.

Holiday pay

A number of recent court decisions have determined what employers must take into account when calculating holiday pay. If you work regular hours and get the same pay each week, holiday pay is simply the same as your normal pay. If your normal pay includes regular bonuses, shift premiums, commission or contractual overtime payments, these should also be included in your holiday pay – voluntary overtime doesn't need to be taken into account, although work-related travel may need to be included in the calculation.

If your weekly pay varies because your hours vary from week to week, your weekly holiday pay should be the average weekly pay you earned over the last 12 weeks. This should include statutory overtime, shift pay and any bonuses.

Holiday pay paid throughout the year

When paid holidays were first introduced in 1998, some people found a change to their pay slip. Their take-home pay was still the same, but it was now made up of two elements. First was their basic pay, which had been reduced from what it had been in previous pay packets. The difference was made up with a second element called holiday pay. The employer then said that there was no need for paid holidays as you were getting your holiday pay through the year and it was up to you to save it up. However, a European Court of Justice case brought by a union in 2006 has made the practice of 'rolling up' holiday pay unlawful.

Changing jobs and holiday rights

You cannot take unused holiday from one job to another. When you leave a job you should get holiday pay for any unused holiday and may have to pay some holiday pay back if you have taken more holiday than you are entitled to.

The amount is worked out using what is called your 'leave year'. This is the period during which you can take your 5.6 weeks' leave. Most workers will have a leave year defined as part of their contract of employment or in a staff handbook, and it will be the same across the organization. Contractual leave years usually start in April or January. If no leave year is defined in this way, your leave year runs between each anniversary of when you started your job.

The amount of holiday you are entitled to for part of a leave year is worked out on an obvious basis. You get one-twelfth of your holiday entitlement for each month you have worked, which is one week's holiday for every three months of your leave year. If you leave after six months and have taken all your four weeks' leave (excluding bank holidays), your employer could make you pay back two weeks' pay. On the other hand, if you have taken no holiday then your employer owes you two weeks' pay.

Days off and breaks

The basic rights are easily stated. You should get at least one day off every week and an uninterrupted break of 11 hours every day. But it does not have to be the same day each week. As an example, your employer can meet the weekly rest requirement by giving you the first day of one week off and the last day of the next week off. This means you can legally work 12 days in a row without a day off, as long as you then get two days off in a row.

Some workers and jobs are treated differently. These include:

- security guards, caretakers and those in other jobs where you need to be there to protect people and property;

- where the job involves travelling long distances;

- where the job requires continuity of service or production, such as hospitals, prisons, docks, airports, media, post and telecommunications, civil protection (such as the police), agriculture, and industries where work cannot be interrupted (eg utilities);

- jobs where there are seasonal rushes, such as tourism, post and agriculture;

- shift workers when they are in the process of changing shift.

The right can also be suspended at any workplace for workers directly involved in dealing with an emergency or accident. However, if you fall into one of these categories, or are faced with an emergency, your employer must provide you with what the regulations call 'compensatory rest' (see page 79). This must provide the same amount of time off, but at a time convenient to the employer.

Breaks at work

You are also entitled to a break of 20 minutes away from where you normally work if your working day is longer than six hours. The same groups of workers who have different provisions for daily and weekly breaks can also have their rest breaks at work varied. Again, if you cannot take your break, you must be given 'compensatory rest' or time off at another time (or 'adequate rest' for transport workers).

In some jobs you may be entitled to longer breaks for health and safety reasons. If your job is particularly repetitive or dangerous (keyboard workers liable to RSI are one example), you may be entitled to more breaks. Take further advice if you are in this position. In a unionized workplace there will normally be a health and safety representative. If not, you can ask the Health and Safety Executive.

Collective and workforce agreements

Provisions in the Working Time Regulations on daily and weekly rest periods, rest breaks at work and the reference period for calculating the average working week can be varied by an agreement between the management and the relevant workforce collectively. However, your boss cannot call you into his or her office and suggest that you give up your breaks, whether it is done politely or with threats of what might happen if you do not. Even through collective agreement you cannot agree to completely give up your entitlement to breaks, because your employer must provide you with an equivalent amount of compensatory rest at a different time.

There are two main ways these agreements can be made. In the regulations these are called collective and workforce agreements. A collective agreement is made between recognized trade unions and management as part of the normal negotiating process. Typically, some sensible flexibility will be agreed in return for some benefit. For example, a different break pattern might be agreed in return for longer breaks. Both sides can benefit from this type of agreement.

A workforce agreement can be made only where there are no recognized unions. The employer will organize an election for workforce representatives, who will then conclude an agreement. This is not a very satisfactory procedure. It is very much under the control of the employer. The representatives who are elected are unlikely to be experts on the WTR, have any training in how to negotiate or be able to call on expert outside advice. Without union back-up workforce representatives are much less likely to get a good deal.

If this is going on in your workplace, you may want to discuss with an appropriate union how best to use it as a way of unionizing your colleagues. At the very least you should make sure that the elected representatives are genuinely independent of the employer and are as briefed as they can be on what the regulations say.

Some minor provisions in your contract of employment can also be varied.

Working out compensatory rest

Even if you fall into one of the categories or there is a collective or workforce agreement that means that you are not covered by some of the rules on breaks, you should still get compensatory rest. This means that you may have to take your breaks or time off at a different time. You can check this by working out how many hours a week in total you are getting as time off, either as breaks at work or between shifts. On average it should be more than 92 hours.

The rules for compensatory rest are not set out in detail, but the government suggests that you should not have to wait more than a couple of weeks for daily rest or more than a couple of months for weekly rest. If you look at your last eight weeks at work and find that you have not had 92 hours' average rest then your employer should be clear about how you can catch up.

The 48-hour working week

The basic right is easily stated – there should be a limit of 48 hours on the maximum average working week. But:

- some jobs are not covered at all or have different rules;
- the 48-hour limit is an average – not a limit – each week;

- the average is calculated in different ways for different types of job;
- individuals and groups of workers can change the way the limit applies or opt out from it altogether.

There are also some real problems defining some of the terms used in the regulations. Many modern (and some older) jobs have grey areas where there is room for argument about whether or not you are actually working.

Defining working time

The basic definition of working time is that you need to be at your workplace and carrying out your working duties under the direction of your employer for it to count as working time. This means that it *does not include*:

- breaks;
- travel to work time, unless you have no fixed base;
- time when you are on call at home but not working;
- training at a college;
- time taken to travel to an occasional meeting away from your normal workplace.

It *does include*:

- overtime;
- training at the workplace provided by your employer;
- time taken travelling to visit clients when this is a regular part of your job, such as for a travelling sales rep or a care worker visiting clients in their homes;
- a working lunch;
- being on call at your place of work.

It can be difficult to define working time for white-collar workers, many of whom regularly work more than 48 hours per week.

It is rare that white-collar workers are told, 'You will stay in the office until 7 pm.' It is more likely to be the pressure of work and peer-group pressure that lead to people working long hours. 'Partly unmeasured working time' does count towards the limits in the WTR. However, employers are still likely to claim that all white-collar work outside the hours set in the contract of employment is voluntary.

Working out your average limit

Some press reporting has suggested that the 48-hour limit applies every week. Except for the special case of night workers involved in dangerous work, this is incorrect. It is always an average limit that, for most people, is calculated over a 17-week reference period. This can be extended up to a maximum of 52 weeks by a collective agreement or workforce agreement if there are objective or technical reasons concerning the organization of work. So even if you work more than 48 hours one week, if you work fewer the next then you may well have worked less than the 48-hour limit on average. To calculate this you need to add up your total working time for each of the last 17 weeks and then divide by 17.

If you were sick or took leave on any days during this period, you should start counting your reference period a week earlier. You should then include enough extra days from the week after the reference period to make up for days that you did not work during the 17 weeks. If there are not enough extra days then you keep starting the reference period earlier until you have enough to get a full 17-week reference period.

There are some exceptions to the 17-week reference period. In some jobs the time over which the average is worked out is extended to 26 weeks. These are the same groups as shown on page 77 who have reduced rights to choose when they take rest breaks. As with rest break rights, employers can switch to a 26-week reference period when there is an emergency. The reference period for offshore workers is 52 weeks.

If you have not yet worked for a full reference period then you calculate the average from when you started work.

It is also possible to vary the reference period by collective or workforce agreement (see page 78). One way it can be varied is to have successive 17-week blocks as the reference periods rather than have a rolling 17-week period. In other words, the first 17 weeks after an agreement was reached could count as the first reference period. Another reference period would then start in week 18.

Another variation that can be made is to extend the reference period. Unions in some workplaces have agreed deals that extend the reference period to a year, providing what is known as an 'annualized hours' contract. This allows companies to respond to seasonal peaks in demand in a flexible way but ensures that employees get extra time off when demand is slack.

Individual opt-outs

At the moment, the 48-hour average limit is the one part of the WTR from which individuals can opt out. You need to do this in writing and you can opt out either for a defined period of time or indefinitely.

But you have the right at any time to opt back in so that you can be covered by the 48-hour average limit once again. The opt-out agreement you signed may have included a time period you have to wait before you are covered again, but this cannot be longer than three months. If there is no time period in your opt-out, you need only wait seven days.

The commonest abuse of the WTR is employers putting undue pressure on their employees to individually opt out of the 48-hour limit. However, they cannot force you to opt out if you do not want to, and they are committing an offence if they dismiss you or treat you less favourably than other employees – what the law calls 'detriment' – because you refuse to opt out. If they do this, you should take advice, as you may have a strong case at an employment tribunal. You will almost certainly get compensation, but you should be aware that, if you get the sack, tribunals only rarely use their power to get people reinstated to their jobs.

However, you are in a trickier position if asked at a job interview whether you will be prepared to opt out and it is apparent to you that this is a condition for getting the job. This is clearly against the spirit of the WTR, but the regulations do not specifically outlaw it.

Once you have started work with an employer, however, and have signed an opt-out, you can give notice to withdraw it at any time. If your employer sacks you at this stage simply for reversing the opt-out, they are breaking the law, and you can take a case to an employment tribunal.

You cannot have your basic pay cut to punish you for refusing to opt out. However, if you are paid by the hour, or receive over-time for hours over your basic working week, you will obviously get more pay if you work more than 48 hours than if you work fewer. There is nothing to stop an employer from paying a higher rate of overtime for hours over 48 hours a week, but if you find your overtime pay has been cut for hours under the 48-hour limit, this may be an illegal variation to your contract of employment. You should take further advice.

Responsibility for enforcing the average 48-hour week limit is shared between the Health and Safety Executive and local authorities. If you do have a problem then you should speak to your union for advice and report the problem to the Pay and Work Rights Helpline: 0300 123 1100.

Night working

Rights for night workers are easily summarized:

- If you regularly work at nights, you should do no more than an average of eight hours in every 24.

- The 48-hour average limit is more strictly regulated, and night workers cannot opt out of the 48-hour average weekly limit (because of the greater threat to health of night work).

- Your employer should provide a free medical check and, where possible, allow you to switch to other shifts on medical advice.

- Young people and those doing especially hazardous work get better protection.

However, as with other working time rights, they are not so straightforward in practice. Some groups are exempt, and the averages for night work limits are calculated in a different way from those for seeing whether you work more than the 48-hour limit.

Defining night work

If you only occasionally work nights, you do not get this protection; only night workers do. To be classed as a night worker you have to work more than three hours at night as part of the normal course of your job. 'At night' means between 11 pm and 6 am. So if you have an evening shift that finishes at 2 am you are a night worker, but if you finish at 1 am you are not as you are only working two hours at night.

However, this definition of 'at night' can be varied by agreement between the employer and the workers by collective and workforce agreements (see page 78). Agreement can also be reached to include more people as night workers, say everyone who works more than two hours during the night period. But there are limits to how much these definitions can be changed. Night time must always be seven hours or more, and it must always include the time between midnight and 5 am.

One of the first court cases decided under the WTR was about the definition of a night worker. The court was asked to rule whether someone who worked one week in three on a night shift was a night worker. The employer argued that the worker was not a night worker as she worked days more often than she worked nights, but lost the case. The court ruled that she was a night worker and said it was the regular nature of her shift pattern that made her a night worker. However, courts have to take account of the particular circumstances of each case, and you cannot therefore rely on this case as setting a definite legal precedent.

Working out the average limit for night work

Night work is worked out as a daily average limit, rather than a weekly limit. It is therefore calculated differently from the 48-hour limit. It is important to appreciate that the average is worked out over the days you can legally work in a week, not the days you actually work. As you are only entitled to a 24-hour rest period each week, this leaves six days when you can legally work.

In other words, you could work nine hours for five nights each week. At first sight this might look as if it breaks the limit of 'a ceiling of an average of eight hours' night work in every 24', but you have to include the sixth night, when you could work even though you are not doing so, when you work out the average.

Let's look at that calculation in detail. Your total working hours in a week are 45. To get the average over six days you divide by six. This gives seven and a half hours. You are therefore not over the limit. If you work exactly the same hours each week, you can use this method to see whether you are over the limit. But if your hours vary it becomes more complex.

The average is always worked out over 17 weeks. However, those groups of workers who have their 'reference period' extended to 26 weeks for working out the 48-hour limit (see page 77) lose night work hours protection altogether rather than have a longer period for working out the average. If you take time off for holidays or sick leave during the 17-week period, you assume that normal hours are worked on those days.

Overtime is only included if it is a regular part of your work and is specified in your contract. If you work only occasional overtime it does not count. If, however, you work overtime every week as part of your normal working pattern, you should include it as part of your total working hours.

If you work different shifts – say one week on nights followed by one week on days – your average night hours will be nowhere near eight hours. We can see why by looking at a two-week period. Say you work five days a week and your night shifts are 10 hours long one week and the day shifts, the next week, are eight hours. Over the two-week period you work 50 hours at night the first week and 40 hours during the day the second week, making 90 hours in all. But over this period there are 12 days when you can legally work nights. However, as you have only done 50 hours of night work during this two-week period the average is 50 ÷ 12, or 4 hours 10 minutes a day. You are still subject to the 48-hour limit – but you are also below this.

Special hazards

If your work involves special hazards or heavy physical or mental strain, and you are a night worker, you cannot work more than eight hours in any 24. This is not an average, but an absolute limit. In other words, as soon as you have worked eight hours you must stop. It therefore does apply to split shift workers when they work nights.

But deciding whether your work is covered by this definition may be trickier. Employers and employees together can agree which jobs are covered through a collective agreement – through either union negotiations or a workforce agreement (see page 78). Your employer is also obliged by law to carry out what is called a risk assessment. As part of this they should decide whether any night workers fall under this category.

Exclusions from the eight-hour limit

Both the eight-hour average and the eight-hour absolute limit can be set aside in the same way that variations can be made to the 48-hour limit by collective agreement (see the section on varying the 48-hour week above).

The eight-hour limit does not apply to these jobs and workers:

- security guards, caretakers and those in other jobs requiring a permanent presence to protect people and property;
- where the job involves travelling long distances;
- where the job requires continuity of service or production, such as hospitals, prisons, docks, airports, media, post and telecommunications, civil protection, and agriculture;
- industries where work cannot be interrupted, such as utilities;
- jobs where there are seasonal rushes, such as tourism, post and agriculture.

Any night worker can lose this protection if his or her job is suddenly affected by an accident, risk of an accident or other unexpected event. But there is no individual opt-out. You cannot sign away your rights. Even if you want to work more than eight hours on average you cannot, unless you are covered by a collective agreement or fall into one of the groups above.

Health checks

Before you begin night work you should be offered a free health assessment. This should be repeated regularly – the government recommends annually. If night work is bad for your health you should, if it is possible for the employer to do so, be offered a chance to transfer to day work.

A health assessment can take the form of a questionnaire, rather than an examination by a doctor or nurse, as long as the questionnaire has been developed by someone medically qualified and is evaluated by someone with training (but not necessarily a doctor or nurse).

Rights for under-18s

If you are over the school leaving age (16) but younger than 18, you are covered by a different set of European regulations – the Young Workers Directive. This was brought into UK law in the WTR. Although your holiday rights are the same as those for older workers, you have different and better rights to breaks.

You should get a continuous break of 12 hours every day (though this can be split in some narrow cases). You should also get a 48-hour continuous break every week (though this can be split in some narrow cases usually involving split shifts, and in some other circumstances limited to 36 hours).

However, as with the 24-hour break enjoyed by older workers, the timing of the break can vary in different weeks. A system where young shop workers got a different two-day break each week would be perfectly legal, for example. You could work 10 days in a row if you had two days' rest at the beginning of the first week and two days off at the end of the second week. In an emergency, and where there is no adult worker available, these breaks can be suspended, but the employer must make them up within three weeks.

Since April 2003 young workers have not been allowed to work more than eight hours per day or 40 hours in a week. Night work is prohibited. Employers can choose whether 'night' means from 10 pm to 6 am or from 11 pm to 7 am.

However, there are still a number of exemptions: young workers may work longer hours if this is necessary to maintain continuity or production, to respond to a surge in demand, or where no adult is available to do this work. In such cases they must be adequately supervised, their training needs must not be adversely affected and they must be allowed compensatory rest. In addition, young workers may work at night in hospitals and similar establishments, and if they are employed in cultural, sporting, artistic or advertising activities. They may also work for part of the night, from 10 or 11 pm until midnight, and from 4 am until 6 or 7 am if they are employed in agriculture, retail trading, a hotel or catering business, restaurants or bars, bakeries, or postal and newspaper deliveries.

Chapter Four
Families and work

Working parents and carers often find it hard to juggle all the competing demands on their time. Much depends on how flexible their employers are prepared to be, but working parents and carers also have some basic rights in law.

Working parents and carers in the UK currently have rights to:

- maternity leave and pay;
- paternity leave and pay;
- adoption leave and pay;
- unpaid parental leave;
- unpaid emergency time off for dependants;
- request flexible working.

These rights apply to people in same-sex and heterosexual relationships and are in addition to the rights of working parents and carers not to suffer unlawful discrimination because of what the law describes as 'protected characteristics', for example sex, pregnancy and maternity, set out in the Equality Act 2010.

Maternity leave

Working mothers have a range of rights both before and after their babies are born. Maternity rights can be complicated to understand – and the law is not always clear. Here we set out your basic rights, but if you get into difficulties you should check with another source – such as your union or an advice agency. There are contact details in Chapter 9. Many employers will provide better rights, which will probably be set out in your contract of employment or staff handbook. They cannot provide a worse deal than the legal minimum even if you have signed a contract that appears to promise less than the law provides.

Pregnancy and maternity leave

Pregnant employees and pregnant agency workers with 12 weeks' service in the same job with the same hirer have the right to paid time off for antenatal care. This is broadly defined and, as well as antenatal appointments, can include relaxation and parent-craft classes, provided they are recommended by a registered midwife or medical practitioner. If your employer unreasonably refuses you time off for antenatal care, or if you don't get paid, you can complain to an employment tribunal. Your employer's actions will also amount to pregnancy and maternity discrimination, but these claims can be complex so you should seek advice. Likewise if you're sacked because you took time off for antenatal care your dismissal will be deemed automatically unfair and you can take a claim to a tribunal. The pregnancy discrimination claim is likely to succeed unless your employer can satisfy the employment tribunal that you were sacked for a reason that had nothing to do with your pregnancy. It doesn't matter how long you have worked for your employer; you are protected from day one in these cases.

A tribunal cannot guarantee that you will get your job back, but there is currently no limit on the amount of compensation a tribunal can award for a successful discrimination claim. You should take advice before bringing a claim from your union or other advice agency.

Maternity leave entitlement

All pregnant employees are entitled to 52 weeks of maternity leave from the day they start work. You can choose when your maternity leave will begin, but the earliest it can start is 11 weeks before the week the baby is due.

Only employees are entitled to maternity leave, so if you are self-employed or an agency worker you won't qualify. The same goes if you are having a child through surrogacy – only the birth mother will qualify for maternity leave, although you may be able to take adoption leave or shared parental leave (see below).

If you are off work for a pregnancy-related reason, such as sickness, in the four weeks before the week in which your baby is due, your employer can insist that your maternity leave start from that date. Some employers don't take this line, though, and will let a woman start her maternity leave as originally planned. If you are disciplined or dismissed because of pregnancy-related sickness absence you can claim pregnancy discrimination in the employment tribunal. Your employer should record pregnancy-related sickness absence separately from other sickness absence.

Every woman who gives birth must have two weeks off (or four if she works in a factory) after the birth. This is compulsory maternity leave and is to protect the health and safety of the mother and the baby.

Giving notice to your employer

In order to qualify for maternity leave you must tell your employer by the end of the 15th week before the baby is due:

- that you are pregnant;
- the week in which your baby is expected; and
- the date when you intend to start your maternity leave.

You are not obliged to put this notice in writing unless your employer asks you to. However, it is probably a good idea to do so, in case any misunderstandings arise in the future. Also, if your employer requests it, you should provide them with a copy of the maternity certificate (MAT B1) given to you by your GP or midwife. If you are unable to give notice by the end of the 15th week before the baby is due, then you must do so as soon as reasonably practicable.

Once you have told your employer you will be taking maternity leave, they then have 28 days to confirm in writing to you the date on which your maternity leave entitlement will end.

Changing the date your maternity leave starts

After you tell your employer when you intend to start your maternity leave, you can change the date. To do so you must tell your employer of the change at least 28 days before the new or original date, whichever is the earlier.

Terms and conditions while on maternity leave

The first 26 weeks of leave are known as ordinary maternity leave (OML), and the subsequent time off (up to an additional 26 weeks) is known as additional maternity leave (AML).

You are entitled to all the same rights under your contract of employment during all of your maternity leave as would apply if you were still at work. The only exception is that you will not be entitled to your normal pay, unless your contract allows for that. Annual leave continues to build up, and you will benefit from any pay increase that may be awarded during your absence. Holidays cannot be carried over from one leave year to the next, so if maternity leave is due to begin partway through the year your employer must allow you to take all your holiday for that year before maternity leave starts or after it ends. Other benefits such as gym membership, childcare vouchers and the use of a company car or phone (unless your contract forbids this) also continue, and there are additional rights if you are made redundant while on maternity leave. Your employer must also pay pension contributions into any occupational pension scheme during your OML and AML when either statutory or contractual maternity pay is paid. Statutory Maternity Pay (SMP) is currently paid to eligible employees for 39 weeks.

Your maternity leave absence counts as continuous employment when deciding whether you are entitled to statutory employment rights such as protection against unfair dismissal.

Returning to work after maternity leave

You have the automatic right to return to work following maternity leave, and it is assumed that you will do so unless you say otherwise:

- You don't have to give your employer notice if you are returning at the end of the full 52 weeks (although it is a good idea to make sure they are expecting you back if they don't contact you).

- If you decide to return to work earlier than the date notified to you by your employer, you must give your employer at least 56 days' (eight weeks') notice that you plan to do so. You do not have to give this notice in writing, although it is advisable to do so and keep a copy.

- Your employer can let you return with less or no notice, although they do not have to, but the most they can make you wait is 56 days (eight weeks) or until the day that your maternity leave was due to end.

- Your employer does not have to pay you if you turn up for work in the meantime.

- If your employer hasn't given you 28 days' notice of the date your maternity leave will end and you turn up for work on the day you thought you were supposed to return, your employer cannot turn you away or fail to pay you if you work.

If you are returning to work after OML, you have a right to return to the same job, seniority, pension and similar rights just as they would have been had you not been on maternity leave. After any AML your employer must allow you to return to the same job unless this is not reasonably practicable (for reasons other than redundancy), in which case you have the right to return to other suitable and appropriate work, again on the same terms and conditions that would have applied had you not taken maternity leave.

If illness prevents you from returning to work

If you are unable to return to work after the end of your maternity leave, you do not lose your right to return but should be treated by your employer as if you have returned to work and are currently on sick leave. You should follow your employer's procedures for sickness absence. Your employer should treat you in the same way as any other employee who is off sick, including paying you any sick pay that is due to you.

If you decide not to return to work after maternity leave

You should resign in the normal way, giving the notice required by your contract or the notice period that is standard in your workplace. If you do not have a contract, or if nothing has been said about how you should resign, you should give a week's notice. You do not have to pay back any SMP you might have received, but you may have to give back any extra pay your employer gave you above the legal minimum.

Other rights

You do have other rights while you are pregnant or on maternity leave:

- Your employer cannot dismiss you or select you for redundancy for any reason connected with pregnancy or maternity.

- You should not be treated unfavourably in other ways when you return – having to work inconvenient shifts or having your job downgraded, for example.

- While you are pregnant, when you have recently given birth and when you are breastfeeding, your employer has to make sure that you are not doing work that would put you or your baby's health and safety at risk.

- If you are planning to breastfeed after you have returned to work then it's a good idea to let your employer know in advance. Your employer should carry out a risk assessment to make sure that breastfeeding at work is safe for both you and the baby.

Keeping in touch during maternity leave

Your employer may have 'reasonable' contact with you during your maternity leave. What is reasonable will depend on the kind of job you do. It is best to agree arrangements for keeping in touch before you go on leave. Your employer must let you know about any promotion opportunities and other important information while you are away.

You are allowed to work up to 10 days during your leave without losing your right to SMP. These are known as keep-in-touch (KIT) days. You cannot be required to work KIT days, nor should you suffer any consequences if you choose not to. If you do decide to work a KIT day, you need to agree whether or not you will be paid – most employers provide a full day's pay – and you should at least receive the minimum wage.

Maternity pay and benefits

The rules on maternity pay can be complex, and if you are not sure of your entitlements you should seek advice. You will get SMP for 39 weeks if you meet all the following conditions:

- You have worked for the same employer for at least 26 weeks by the end of the 15th week before your child is due (this is called the *qualifying week*).

- You are still in your job in this qualifying week (it does not matter if you are off sick or on holiday).

- You earn at least the Lower Earnings Limit (before tax) per week on average in the eight weeks (if you are paid weekly) or two months up to the last payday before the end of the qualifying week.

If you meet these conditions, you are entitled to 90 per cent of your average pay in the first six weeks of maternity leave, and then you will receive the basic rate of SMP for the next 33 weeks, unless your employer is more generous. Some are, especially where unions are recognized, because often maternity agreements providing higher contractual maternity pay have been reached.

You should still get SMP even if you leave employment or are made redundant before your maternity leave has started. If you leave or are made redundant after SMP has started, your employer must pay you for the full 39 weeks.

If you work for an agency you can claim SMP but only if you have been employed by the agency throughout the entire 26-week period leading up to the qualifying week. This is the case even if you are sent by the agency to a different workplace every day or if you didn't work at all during the 26 weeks, but of course your earnings must not drop below the Lower Earnings Limit and you must have told the agency that you're pregnant.

Maternity Allowance (MA)

If you are not entitled to SMP, you may still be entitled to MA if you have worked for a total of 26 weeks in the 66 weeks before the week your baby is due (these need not be consecutive weeks). However, you will need to meet some complex earnings conditions and should seek advice from the Department for Work and Pensions or Jobcentre Plus, who will work out how much you should get.

Other benefits

If you are not entitled to SMP or MA, you may be entitled to other benefits such as Employment and Support Allowance, and you could also qualify for Working Tax Credits and Child Tax Credits. The Sure Start Maternity Grant is available to women on low incomes who don't have any other children aged under 16 years in the family. You should contact Jobcentre Plus, GOV.UK or a specialist adviser who will be able to tell you whether you qualify.

Paternity leave

If you're becoming a father or your partner or spouse is giving birth or adopting a child then you may be entitled to take two weeks of paternity leave. This leave is designed to help with the early stages of looking after the child, and can be taken within 56 days of the child being born or being placed in your care. It is available to both same-sex and opposite-sex partners.

Paternity leave entitlement

Where the mother or your partner is giving birth

To qualify for paternity leave you must have been continuously employed by your current employer for 26 weeks or more by the end of the 15th week before the child is due – this is known as the *qualifying week*. To be eligible for paternity leave you must be the biological father, adoptive parent, spouse or partner of the mother or her civil partner, and expected to share the main responsibility for raising the child.

Where your partner is adopting

To qualify for paternity leave you must have been continuously employed by your current employer for 26 weeks or more in the week after the week that your partner is notified that they have been matched with a child – this is known as the *qualifying week*. You must be the spouse, partner or civil partner of the person who is adopting the child and expect to have the main responsibility, along with them, for the child's upbringing.

Giving notice to your employer

Where your partner is giving birth

In the 15th week before the child is expected, you must tell your employer the week that the child is due, how much leave you intend to take (you can take either one week or two consecutive weeks) and the date that you intend the leave to start. There may be cases where it is not possible to give this much notice, for example if a child is born prematurely or a pregnancy is discovered very late. In these circumstances you are allowed to give notice as soon as 'reasonably practicable'.

Your employer can ask to see self-certificate form SC3, 'Becoming a parent', which confirms that you meet all the criteria and so are entitled to take the leave (forms are available from GOV.UK and can be downloaded from their website **www.gov.uk**), but you only have to give them this certificate if they ask you to. You should make sure you have a copy of it, so that both you and your employer are clear about when your leave will start and end. Once your child has been born, you must tell your employer.

Where your partner is adopting a child

In the week following the week in which your partner is told that they have been matched with a child, you must tell your employer: the date that your partner was notified; the date that you are expecting the child to be placed with you; and the date that you want your paternity leave to start. In some cases there might not be time to give this notice, in which case you must give your employer notice as soon as reasonably practicable.

Your employer can ask to see self-certificate form SC4, 'Becoming an adoptive parent', which will confirm that you are entitled to take paternity leave, but you only have to give this to them if they ask. If you do give it to them, keep a copy so that both you and your employer are clear about the dates that your leave will start and end. Once the placement has been made, you must inform your employer of this. Self-certificate form SC4 can be downloaded from **www.gov.uk**.

Changing the date your paternity leave starts

Even after you have agreed dates for your leave, you can still change your mind as long as you notify your employer of the change at least 28 days before the new date, or as soon as is reasonably practicable. Your paternity leave will then start on this new date.

Employment terms and conditions while on paternity leave

While on paternity leave, you continue with the same terms and conditions except for pay. This is still the case if you take paternity leave and follow it with annual leave or parental leave of less than four weeks (parental leave is discussed later in this chapter).

Returning to work

You are entitled to return to the same job that you had before you went on leave and to benefit from the same conditions that you would have received had you not been on leave. This is the case if you took two or more weeks' paternity leave on its own, or linked it with statutory leave such as annual leave or less than four weeks of parental leave.

If you take 26 weeks' additional paternity leave combined with more than four weeks' parental leave, you are allowed to return to the job you were doing before you went on leave or, if your employer can argue that this is not reasonably practicable, you should be given another job that is appropriate for you to do in the circumstances.

Statutory Paternity Pay (SPP)

You will get SPP if you meet all the following conditions:

- You have worked for the same employer for at least 26 weeks by the end of the 15th week before your child is due or the week in which your partner was notified of being matched with a child for adoption.

- You are still in your job in this qualifying week (it does not matter if you are off sick or on holiday).

- You earn at least the Lower Earnings Limit (before tax) per week on average in the eight weeks (if you are paid weekly) or two months up to the last payday before the end of the qualifying week.

If you do meet these criteria, you are entitled to receive £139.58 (for 2015/16), or 90 per cent of your average weekly earnings if this is less. If you are unsure about whether you qualify for paternity pay and leave, it is important that you seek expert advice.

Adoption leave

If you are adopting a child you are entitled to take up to 52 weeks' adoption leave provided you give proper notice and you meet the eligibility criteria.

In order to get adoption leave you must have been continuously employed by the same employer for 26 weeks or more in the week that you are told you have been matched with a child. This is known as your *qualifying week*. You must be the person adopting the child (in a couple, only one parent can take adoption leave), and you must have notified the adoption agency that you agree to the placement.

Different rules apply if you are adopting from overseas.

Giving notice

You must tell your employer that you want to take adoption leave within seven days of being told by the adoption agency that you have been matched with a child. You must specify the date on which the child is expected to be placed with you and the date that you have chosen your leave period to start.

Unlike maternity leave, which cannot begin until the 11th week before the week the child is expected, adoption leave cannot begin earlier than 14 days before the date on which the child will be placed with you for adoption.

Your employer can ask for your notice in writing and for evidence that you are entitled to take adoption leave. To provide this you must make available: the name and address of the adoption agency; the name and date of birth of the child; the date that you were told that you had been matched with the child; and the date that the agency intends to place the child in your care. This documentary evidence can take the form of a *matching certificate*, which may be available from the adoption agency and is available from GOV.UK at **www.gov.uk**. It always makes sense to put these kinds of request in writing and keep copies.

Once you have given your notice, your employer has 28 days to tell you the date on which your adoption leave will finish.

Changing when your adoption leave starts

Once you have told your employer when you intend to start your adoption leave you can change this date. To do this you must tell your employer of the variation at least 28 days before the new date, or as soon as is reasonably practicable. Again, it is best to do this in writing.

Terms and conditions while on adoption leave

While you are on adoption leave all of your terms and conditions are protected, except for pay. You will keep your normal employment rights and benefits such as a company car or mobile phone.

If your employer contributes into a pension scheme for you they must continue to do so the whole time you are on ordinary adoption leave (OAL), which is the first 26 weeks, during any time that you are receiving Statutory Adoption Pay (SAP; eligible employees are currently entitled to 39 weeks' SAP) and during any time that you are receiving contractual adoption pay. So if your contract provides for adoption pay throughout the entire 52 weeks of leave your employer must make pension contributions on your behalf throughout. If your contract doesn't entitle you to adoption pay after 39 weeks of SAP, your employer doesn't have to make any employer contributions to your pension scheme for the remaining 13 weeks of additional adoption leave (AAL).

If you normally make pension contributions, you should carry on doing so during your adoption leave absence. Unpaid AAL leave does not count as pensionable service but does not interrupt your continuity of service, and the periods of time either side of the AAL period will be treated as continuous.

You will continue to build up holiday entitlement during both OAL and AAL. This applies to any contractual holiday entitlement as well, but you can't take statutory paid holiday at the same time as adoption leave. You may, however, be able to take holiday at the end of adoption leave if your employer agrees.

Your period of adoption leave also counts as continuous employment for building up statutory employment rights such as protection against unfair dismissal. Your employer is entitled to maintain 'reasonable' contact with you while you are on adoption leave. Arrangements are the same as for mothers on maternity leave. Some of this can be quite complicated, and you should seek advice from your trade union representative or a specialist adviser.

Returning to work after adoption leave

You have the automatic right to return to work following adoption leave, and it is assumed that you will do so unless you say otherwise:

- You don't have to tell your employer if you are returning at the end of the full 52 weeks (although it is a good idea to make sure they are expecting you back if they don't contact you).

- If you decide to return to work earlier than the date specified by your employer, you must give them 56 days' notice of your intention to do so. You do not have to give this notice in writing, although it is advisable that you do and keep a copy.

- Your employer can let you return earlier, although they do not have to, but the most they can make you wait is 56 days or until the day that your adoption leave was due to end.

- Your employer does not have to pay you if you turn up for work in the meantime.

If you are returning to work after OAL (the first 26 weeks), you have a right to return to the same job. If you return after a period of AAL (ie more than 26 weeks' leave), your employer is obliged to provide suitable employment if it is not reasonably practicable for you to return to your old job.

If illness prevents you from returning to work

If you cannot return to work on the agreed date, you do not lose your right to return. Instead, your employer should treat you as if you had returned to work but are now on sick leave. You must therefore follow your employer's sickness procedures. Your employer should treat you in the same way as any other employee who is off sick, including paying you any sick pay to which you're entitled.

If you decide not to return to work after adoption leave

You should resign in the normal way, giving the notice required by your contract or that is standard in your workplace. If you do not have a contract, or if nothing has been said about how you should resign, you should give a week's notice. You do not have to pay back any SAP you have received, but you may have to give back any extra pay your employer gave you above the statutory minimum.

Other rights

You do have other rights when you are on adoption leave:

- Your employer cannot dismiss you or select you for redundancy for any reason connected with the adoption.
- You should not be treated unfavourably when you go back to work – having to work inconvenient shifts or having your job downgraded, for example.

Statutory Adoption Pay

You may be entitled to receive SAP while you are on adoption leave. You will receive SAP if you:

- are matched with a child by a UK adoption agency;
- have been continuously employed by the same employer for at least 26 weeks before the week that you are told you have been matched with a child (it does not matter if you are off sick or on holiday during this time);
- earn at least the Lower Earnings Limit (before tax) per week on average in the eight weeks (if you are paid weekly) or two months (if you are paid monthly) up to the last payday before the week after the week you were notified of the child's placement.

You must also provide your employer with the same information that you need to give to trigger adoption leave, contained in the matching certificate described on page 102. You only have to submit it once to your employer, but you must do so at least 28 days before the date that you have chosen for your pay period to start, or as soon as is reasonably practicable. If you are in a relationship, your partner may be able to receive paternity pay and paternity leave. However, an individual cannot be in receipt of both statutory adoption *and* statutory paternity pay.

If you qualify for SAP, you will receive either the basic rate (currently £139.58 a week) or 90 per cent of your average weekly earnings if they are less than the basic rate, for 39 weeks. If you do not qualify for SAP, you may be entitled to other benefits and should contact Jobcentre Plus for this information. Jobcentre Plus information is local, and their contact details can be found in your local telephone directory. See Chapter 9 for contact details for GOV.UK and Citizens Advice Bureaux.

New rights to shared parental leave

From 5 April 2015, parents in the UK have been allowed to share leave following the birth or adoption of a child. The right extends to couples in paid work, including parents, adopters, same-sex couples and cohabiting couples. Those who are eligible can take up to 50 weeks of maternity or adoption leave as shared parental leave (SPL) and can take up to 37 weeks of maternity or adoption pay as shared parental pay.

SPL doesn't have to be a single continuous period; leave periods can be as little as a week, and both parents can be absent from work at the same time.

There's been no change to maternity or adoption leave. Mothers and adopters still have the right to take up to 52 weeks' leave, only now you also have the option of swapping maternity or adoption leave for SPL, to be taken by your partner.

You have the right to SPL if your expected week of childbirth (EWC) began on or after 5 April 2015 or a child was placed for adoption with you on or after that date.

Leave may be taken at any time between the end of compulsory maternity leave (two weeks after the birth) and a day before the child's first birthday. It has to be taken in complete weeks either as one continuous period or in shorter periods.

If you're adopting, leave can be taken from the first day the child is placed with you and will end a day before the first anniversary.

Who is eligible to take shared parental leave?

Self-employed parents and agency workers won't be able to take shared parental leave, but their partners might be able to.

As the person who will take the shared parental leave, you must have worked for the same employer for 26 weeks by the end of the 15th week before the baby is due (or by the date you are matched with your adopted child). You must still be working for the same employer right up to the day you take SPL.

Giving notice

Both you and your partner must sign notices of entitlement and intention to take SPL.

As the mother or adopter wishing to share parental leave with your partner, you must give your employer eight weeks' notice of your intention to 'curtail' your maternity or adoption leave. You can do this by returning to work, but you will have to give notice to do that anyway.

Notice has to be given in writing and include the (earlier) date on which your ordinary maternity or adoption leave will end. The same goes if you intend to share your additional maternity or adoption leave. However, the date must be at least one week before the day on which your additional maternity or adoption leave was due to end.

The partner of the mother or adopter must meet the requirements of the 'employment and earnings test', which means having worked on an employed or self-employed basis for 26 weeks of the last 66 weeks, earning at least £30 per week on average for 13 of those weeks.

Statutory Shared Parental Pay

How much shared parental pay you will be entitled to receive depends on how you decide to share the leave between yourselves, taking into account the amount of maternity leave, maternity pay or allowance, adoption leave or adoption pay you may also be receiving.

The current Statutory Shared Parental Pay rate is £139.58 per week or 90 per cent of your average weekly earnings, whichever is lower.

Other rights

Your employer cannot dismiss you or select you for redundancy for any reason connected with SPL.

You should not be treated unfavourably when you go back to work – having to work inconvenient shifts or having your job downgraded, for example.

Unpaid parental leave

If you are an employee and have worked for your employer for at least a year, you currently have the right to take 18 weeks' unpaid parental leave to care for each child and adopted child.

You are not entitled to unpaid parental leave if you are self-employed, an agency worker or a contractor. Some workplaces will have special agreements for parental leave that have been reached between the employer and the union or other workplace representative. For instance, the agreement might set out how and when you can take your leave or it might include some payment for employees taking parental leave. You should check whether any such scheme applies where you work, as it will override the basic state scheme.

If your employer does not provide a parental leave payment, you may still qualify for tax credits and benefits. You should consult your local benefits agency and GOV.UK. You can also speak to a specialist adviser such as a Citizens Advice Bureau if you are unsure about benefits and tax credits.

You qualify for unpaid parental leave if you are an adoptive parent, have parental responsibility for a child, or your name is on the child's birth certificate. Unlike in the case of paid holiday, your employer cannot tell you when to take parental leave, but they can postpone it.

Entitlement

You can take 18 weeks' leave for each child up to the child's 18th birthday. You must take the leave in week-long blocks unless your employer agrees otherwise or the child is in receipt of Disability Living Allowance (DLA), in which case you can take it in blocks of a day. You cannot take more than four weeks in any one year for any one child, but if you have more than one child you can take four weeks per year per child. The entitlement to parental leave is per child and is limited to 18 weeks regardless of whether you are with the same employer when you take it. So, if you qualify for parental leave and take four weeks' leave and then move jobs, you will only be entitled to take a further 14 weeks' leave (per child) once you have reached the qualifying period with your new employer. If during this time your child reaches his or her 18th birthday, you lose your entitlement to parental leave for that child.

Giving notice

You must give your employer 21 days' notice if you want to take unpaid parental leave, and you must specify the dates when you intend your leave to start and finish. You are not obliged to put this notice in writing, but it is often a good idea to do so in case there is any confusion later.

Giving notice of leave that starts with the birth of a child

If you are a parent-to-be wanting to take leave from the date of the birth, you should give notice at least 21 days before the beginning of the anticipated week of the birth. You should say when the baby is due and how much leave you want to take once the baby is born. Provided you have given this notice, you can start your parental leave as soon as the baby is born, regardless of whether the birth is earlier or later than was expected.

However, you may decide to take paid paternity leave instead of or as well as unpaid parental leave. You are required to give *28 days' notice* for paternity leave and so, if you decide to take paternity leave immediately following a period of parental leave, you should be aware of the different notice requirements and act accordingly. If you are unsure of what to do, you should seek advice. Good employers will provide this information. You can also take parental leave in combination with adoption leave. Take care to follow the notice requirements for each.

Postponement

If an employer thinks that your absence would unduly disrupt the business, they can delay your parental leave, but for no more than six months after the date that you originally gave. Your employer has to tell you this in writing within seven days of the day you give them notice of your intention to take parental leave, and they have to give you a reason. Your employer cannot postpone your leave entitlement a second time, even if they feel that their reasons for refusing the leave in the first instance have not changed. If you think that your employer has unreasonably postponed your parental leave or prevented you from taking it, you can take your case to an employment tribunal. You would have to make your complaint within three months. If this situation occurs, you should seek advice immediately from your union representative or an advice agency.

Returning to work

If you take leave for four weeks or less, you have the right to return to the same job you did before. This is the case if you take parental leave following a different form of statutory leave such as paternity leave, *ordinary* maternity leave or *ordinary* adoption leave.

However, if you take more than four weeks' parental leave on its own, or combined with *additional* maternity leave or *additional* adoption leave, you have the right to return to the same job unless your employer can show that it is not reasonably practicable to let you do this. If this is the case, you are entitled to come back to another job that is both suitable and appropriate for you.

Terms and conditions while on parental leave

During parental leave you will still be an employee, but your employer is not obliged to pay your wages during that time. Your contractual rights, such as the right to 28 days' paid annual leave, will not be affected and can still build up while you are on parental leave. You are also entitled to benefit from any pay increases or improvements to other terms and conditions introduced (or taking effect) during your absence.

If you took parental leave *before* 6 April 2003, your employer can leave out the time that you were on leave when calculating seniority or pensionable service. The time spent on parental leave will not count as time employed, but the period of employment before the leave period will be treated as continuous with that following your return to work. However, for employees who have taken parental leave *after* 6 April 2003, periods of parental leave must be counted for purposes of seniority, pension and similar rights. In these circumstances the employee will be treated as if he or she had never been absent.

The other contractual rights that continue automatically are:

- the notice period stated in your contract – you or your employer should still give this amount of notice if either of you wants to end your job contract;

- your right to redundancy pay if you are made redundant;

- procedures for grievance or disciplinary action;

- any terms and conditions preventing you from working for competing organizations or disclosing confidential information about your employer's business.

Who has parental responsibility?

Natural mothers and married fathers automatically have parental responsibility for a child. Unmarried fathers will have parental responsibility if they have been granted this by the mother or through a court order. For parental leave, an unmarried father whose name appears on his child's birth certificate automatically has parental responsibility. Adoptive parents usually get parental responsibility when the adoption order is made. Same-sex partners and others may sometimes get parental responsibility through legal proceedings.

If your employer is disputing your right to take leave on any of these grounds, you should seek legal advice.

Protection

Your employer must not discriminate against you or treat you unfairly because you apply for or take leave, and if they do you may be able to take a claim to an employment tribunal. If you are dismissed because you asked to take, or took, parental leave, you may be able to claim unfair dismissal.

Some employers give new parents more than the legal minimum of maternity, paternity and adoption leave. If your employer tries to deduct this extra amount from your 18 weeks' parental leave, they could be in breach of your contract, and in certain cases could be guilty of sex discrimination. If any of these problems arise, you should seek advice from your union or a legal specialist.

Flexible working rights for parents and carers

All employees have a right in law to ask their employer to work flexibly provided they have worked for their employer for

26 weeks continuously on the date the application is made. The right doesn't apply to agency workers and office holders.

Flexible working can include changing your hours, the times when these hours are worked and where you are required to work.

Many employers already operate flexible working arrangements, and to find out your entitlement you need to check your contract of employment, your staff handbook, or any special leaflet that the personnel department may provide in larger organizations.

Improving benefits and entitlements on flexible working is a priority for unions, so if you work for an organization that recognizes unions you are very likely to have access to more generous flexible working arrangements.

Arrangements for flexible working set out in your contract of employment may be legally binding, which means that your employer must honour them because they have been promised to you. If you have a dispute over your terms and conditions on flexible working, you should seek specialist advice.

The concept of flexible working is very wide, and you could ask for a variety of different work patterns or arrangements under these new rights. These include:

- working from home;
- job-sharing;
- teleworking;
- term-time working;
- compressed hours;
- flexitime;
- staggered hours;
- annualized hours;
- self-rostering.

How to make a request

You must comply with the following rules when making a request. Your application must:

- be made in writing, in either paper or electronic form, stating that it is being made under the statutory right to apply for flexible working;

- set out your proposed change to your working patterns and explain what effect you think this change would have on your employer and how this might be dealt with;

- state whether you have made a previous application under this right and, if so, the date on which it was made;

- be dated.

Your employer must, by law, handle your request in a reasonable manner.

If your request is granted, the terms and conditions of your contract are varied to take account of that change. Unless otherwise agreed, changes to your contract are permanent and *you have no right to revert to your previous terms and conditions*. You should get advice about this from your union representative, if you have one, or a legal adviser. You may want to consider asking for the flexible arrangements to apply for a short time only, eg until the health of an elderly parent improves, with the option of going back to your original working pattern on giving your employer reasonable notice.

What happens after I make my request?

Once a request has been made your employer should discuss it with you as soon as possible and let you know if there's likely to be any delay in considering your request. The whole process, including any appeal, shouldn't take longer than three months. Time to consider your request can be extended beyond three months as long as you agree.

The discussion with your employer doesn't have to be face to face; a telephone call or exchange of e-mails is fine as long as you agree to it. Where a meeting has been arranged, as a matter of good practice your employer should offer you the option of being accompanied at the meeting by your trade union representative or a work colleague and give you enough time, before the meeting, to arrange for the representative or colleague to attend.

If you can't attend on the suggested date, your employer should reschedule the meeting. If, for any reason, you can't attend on the date arranged, you should notify your employer. If you simply don't show, the law allows your employer to treat your application as withdrawn.

Business grounds for your employer refusing your request

Your employer must handle your request for flexible working in a reasonable manner. They may turn down your request for flexible working only on one or more of a number of 'business' grounds. These are:

- burden of additional costs;
- detrimental effect on the ability to meet customer demand;
- inability to reorganize work among existing staff;
- inability to recruit additional staff;
- detrimental impact on quality;
- detrimental impact on performance;
- insufficiency of work during the periods the employee proposes to work;
- planned structural changes.

If your employer turns down your request either initially or after an appeal hearing, they should notify you of this in writing and/or discuss the decision with you.

Going to an employment tribunal

If your request has been rejected on appeal, you may be able to complain to an employment tribunal if you can show that your request was refused for a reason other than one of the prescribed business reasons. For example, where the flexible working arrangements would be a reasonable adjustment for a disabled employee, refusing a request could give rise to a claim of disability discrimination. Similarly, where flexible working is required for reasons of child or other caring responsibilities, your employer's refusal may be indirectly discriminatory. Discrimination claims can be difficult to prove, so you should contact your union or an advice agency if you think you may have a claim.

Employment tribunal fees

In July 2013, the government introduced fees for all claims in employment tribunals and employment appeal tribunals. There are two types of claims, which dictate the level of fees to be paid:

- Type A claims include those for unpaid wages, payment in lieu of notice and redundancy payments. The issue fee is £160, and the hearing fee is £230.
- Type B claims include unfair dismissal, discrimination complaints, equal pay and whistle-blowing claims. The issue fee is £250, and the hearing fee is £950.

If you cannot afford to pay, you may be eligible for a full or partial waiver of fees under the HM Courts & Tribunals Service fee remissions scheme, eg if you are in receipt of certain state benefits.

Afterwards, if you want to appeal a decision in an employment appeal tribunal there are more fees: £400 to start the appeal and £1,200 for the hearing itself.

What happens if I don't pay and don't apply for remission?

If you don't pay the fee or make an application for remission, the tribunal will send you a notice telling you the date by which you must pay (or make a remission application), and if you fail to pay by the date specified then your claim will not be allowed to proceed.

Fees for more than one claim

If you wish to bring several claims at the same time you only need to pay one issue fee and one hearing fee. If they include both type A and type B claims, eg unpaid wages and unfair dismissal, then the higher fee (for type B claims) will be payable.

Claims brought by a group of employees

If you are one of several employees at the same workplace affected by the same or a similar issue, eg overtime and holiday pay, different levels of fees apply depending on the numbers involved.

Recovering fees

Winning your claim does not necessarily mean you will be entitled to recover all fees paid. However, you can ask the tribunal to order your employer to reimburse your fees. If your claim is settled before going to tribunal you might be able to recover the fees from your employer as part of the agreement to settle.

Changes ahead?

As anticipated, the introduction of fees has seen a reduction year on year (by over 70 per cent) in the number of claims lodged in the tribunal. In June 2015 the government announced a review of the fees regime, the aim of which is to see whether the original objectives of reducing costs and encouraging other ways to resolve workplace disputes, while maintaining access to justice, have been met.

Time off for dependants

All employees have the right to 'reasonable' time off work to help people such as family members or friends who depend on them for assistance in an emergency. There is no set limit on how much time off can be taken, but you can only take off the time necessary to sort out the immediate problem.

Your employer can stop your pay while you are away, even if the leave is just a few hours. However, some employers (often those with trade union agreements on 'family', 'special' or 'carers'' leave) may give paid leave in these circumstances, perhaps up to a certain number of days per year.

What is a dependant?

A dependant means your parent, wife, husband, partner or civil partner or child, or someone else who lives with you as part of your family. It does not include someone in a more commercial relationship with you, such as a live-in employee or a tenant. A 'dependant' can also be someone who 'reasonably' relies on you for help if he or she is ill or has an accident, or when his or her normal care arrangements have broken down (for example, this could apply to a neighbour or friend of yours with a disability).

Qualifying circumstances

An employee has the right to reasonable time off to deal with an emergency or other unforeseen event, for example:

- to help when a dependant falls ill, gives birth, is injured or is assaulted (the definition of illness and injury includes mental illness or injury);
- when a dependant dies;
- to cope when the arrangements for caring for a dependant unexpectedly break down;

- to cope with an unexpected incident involving a dependent child during school hours or on a school trip, or in other circumstances when the school has responsibility for the child.

Employees relying on this right must tell their employer as soon as reasonably practicable why they are absent and (unless they are already back at work) how long the absence is likely to last. This leave is for emergencies or unexpected incidents rather than events that can be predicted. You are expected to take a different form of leave in the latter circumstances.

The right to time off for dependants depends, to a large extent, on what is *reasonable*, and this is not defined in law. Therefore, it can be difficult to know where you stand if your employer refuses to grant you leave or says that you took leave without authority. In this situation you should consult your union representative or a specialist adviser immediately.

These leave rights do not apply to other domestic emergencies such as break-ins, fire or floods, although most employers should be reasonable in such circumstances.

Chapter Five
Common problems at work

In a well-run workplace it should be possible to resolve problems without involving any legal procedures. Responsible employers will not only have proper internal procedures but also foster the kind of environment where it is possible to raise issues informally. Good employers recognize that if their staff have grievances and other problems they are unlikely to give their best.

But things can go wrong in even the best-run workplaces. Responsible employers may have good policies, but a bullying manager in a branch office may ignore them all. Of course, you should make every effort to resolve issues informally if it is possible. You can talk to your boss or, if the boss is the problem, your personnel or human resources department. If you have one, your union representative may well be able to sort out many problems on an informal basis.

In this chapter we look at some of the commonest problems where the law sets standards or could have a role in resolving a problem. These are health and safety, stress, bullying, drink, drugs, smoking and problems with your contract. We end by explaining how the law regulates formal procedures for resolving grievances or disciplinary matters at work.

Health and safety

You have a right to work in a healthy and safe environment. There are tough laws to ensure that your rights in this respect are safeguarded. While there is always room for improvement and a glaring need for more resources for enforcement – as some high-profile cases sometimes remind us – the UK is generally recognized as having a relatively effective health and safety regime. However, while most large companies will understand their responsibilities, this is not always the case in smaller companies. And any death or injury at work is one too many.

Under the Health and Safety at Work Act 1974 your employer must ensure that nothing that happens at work makes you ill or injures you (this is known as the 'duty of care'). This could involve guarding machinery, making sure chemicals you work with are safe and ensuring that you can take breaks when you are tired. It even includes providing adequate canteen and toilet facilities.

Every employer must have a health and safety policy, explaining how they will manage health and safety, and who is responsible for what. Your employer must identify the hazards you might face at work, assess the risk these hazards pose and detail the steps that will be taken to prevent those risks.

Many people are confused by the specific legal use of these terms in health and safety. Basically, a *hazard* is something that could cause you harm, and a *risk* is the likelihood of harm arising from the hazard. Hazards can be physical (scaffolding or repetitive work, for example), chemical (eg asbestos or isocyanates), biological (eg tuberculosis) or psychosocial (eg stress).

Under the Act you must cooperate with the steps taken by your employer to protect health and safety in the workplace, to the extent that you are able. So if your employer tells you to work in a certain way because it is safer they must make it possible for you to do as they say, and you should follow their instructions.

You must not endanger fellow workers by your actions or omissions. Basically, this means that you should follow the safety procedures laid down by your managers where they have given you the appropriate tools and resources. You should also avoid anything that might be seen as 'horseplay' or 'pranks' that could go wrong and cause injury or illness.

There are also 'implied' rights and duties in your contract of employment (see the Introduction), which can be important in any tribunal or court case. Again, there is a basic duty for your employer to provide a safe and healthy workplace, and for you to pay proper regard in the workplace to your own and your colleagues' health and safety.

No goggles provided

Sheila Robinson and her fellow employees were required to wear eye protectors while at work. Sheila was given goggles, but they were no use because she had to wear glasses. She complained to the safety officer, and he said that he would approach the company to see if they would pay for special eye protectors fitted with Sheila's prescription lenses. She heard nothing more about the matter and after more than a year decided that she was left with no alternative but to resign.

Sheila claimed that she had been constructively dismissed and that the dismissal was unfair. She won, though only after an appeal. The employment appeal tribunal (EAT) ruled that the employer was in breach of their common law duty to take reasonable care for the safety of employees. It was held that this general duty included an obligation to act promptly and reasonably in dealing with safety questions or complaints. It was found that there was no good reason for the employer's failure to respond to the complaint, and so the constructive dismissal was found to be unfair.

Everyone is covered

Statutory health and safety rights are not limited to employees (see the Introduction for the difference between employees and other legal categories of worker). Anyone present in the workplace is covered, whether they are employees or a workers – including agency and subcontracted workers. Even visitors and others not directly under the control of the employer are protected.

A special government agency called the Health and Safety Executive (HSE) polices health and safety. If an injury occurs or if workers, unions or members of the public raise serious concerns with the HSE, it will investigate and can order changes to be made. As a final resort it can close a dangerous workplace down and prosecute employers in the criminal courts.

In addition, if you are injured at work because of a failure by your employer to maintain proper standards you can claim compensation in a civil action. Employers must also be insured against such claims.

Your employer must provide you with information about the risks and hazards of your work, and what they intend to do about them. They must provide you with training (at no cost to you) in how to work safely, and keep your training up to date.

Hazardous chemicals are required by law to come with a safety data sheet setting out what the hazards are, and what can be done to prevent illness and injury. The supplier is legally obliged to supply these sheets to your employer.

What your employer must do

Every employer must conduct a risk assessment, and then follow a legally binding 'hierarchy of control', which lays down the order in which various steps should be taken to deal with risks to their staff or anyone else at their workplace. This hierarchy is laid out in the Management of Health and Safety at Work Regulations 1999.

Firstly, the source of the risk should be replaced. For example, different machinery, chemicals or processes could be introduced.

Secondly, and only if the first option is not possible or 'reasonably practicable', the source of the risk should be isolated from you and your fellow workers. For example, it could be put in a sealed room, or guards could be put on machinery.

Thirdly, if the first two steps cannot be taken, the risk should be minimized, by using less of a substance, or reducing the time you are exposed to the risk.

Lastly, if all else fails, the employer should provide you with personal protective equipment (such as ear-plugs, overalls and breathing apparatus).

Most health and safety law requires employers to take all the steps that are 'reasonably practicable'. This means that they do not have to use a sledgehammer to crack a nut. But it does not mean that if it costs money they do not have to do it, and it does not even mean that if they cannot afford it they do not have to do it. In practice, most health and safety measures pay for themselves in reduced accidents, reduced sick pay and reduced compensation payments.

At a minimum, your employer must:

- maintain plant and work systems safely;
- ensure that risks to health and safety are avoided when using, handling, storing or transporting substances or articles;
- provide information, training and supervision to ensure the health and safety of workers;
- maintain safe access to and from the workplace;
- prepare a statement of general policy on health and safety;
- ensure that minimum standards are met and bring these to workers' attention;
- ensure that there are workforce safety representatives and consult them so that they can assist in establishing and maintaining health and safety standards;
- set up a safety committee to review arrangements if the safety representatives request this.

If a union is recognized in your workplace the safety representatives will be chosen through union channels. Where there is no union, it is up to the employer to ensure that they consult the workforce by other means.

Where unions are fully involved in the workplace health and safety system serious injury rates fall by more than 50 per cent. Whenever your employer does something that could affect your health and safety they are required by law to consult either your safety representative or the workers who are affected. This consultation must be genuine – it must be 'in good time' (legal jargon that means it cannot be left so late that there would be no time to make changes as a result of the consultation), and your employer must take account of your response.

Where there is union recognition, unions can appoint safety representatives who have: a right to time off for union training; a right to be consulted and to represent their fellow workers; a right to investigate accidents; and a right to be involved in inspections by the HSE or local environmental health officers. They can also require joint union–management safety committees to be set up, which have the backing of the national union – providing them with access to information and back-up.

If you have a problem at work regarding health and safety, the first person to contact should be your supervisor or manager. If you are not satisfied with the response or are unsure about your position or what to do, contact your safety representative. You should be given his or her name and location when you join the company, probably in a staff handbook or attachment to your contract of employment, and it will most likely be posted up somewhere on a notice board.

Special hazards

In addition to these general rights and responsibilities there are many detailed rules and regulations about particular hazards that will affect different workplaces or occupations, such as offshore oil or quarrying. These cover issues such as handling particular chemicals, working with particular machinery, noise at work, or risk of electric shock. Normally there is a duty to display these regulations or make them available. Although they are often in rather heavy legal language and usually presented in extremely dull small print, it is worth studying them.

Some of the areas covered by specific legislation (or where legislation is being considered) are:

- *Back strain:* The Manual Handling Regulations cover most hazards to the back, including heavy lifting (although there are no maximum weights), and the Display Screen Equipment Regulations cover back problems caused by visual display units (VDUs).

- *Stress:* The general duties of employers to care for their employees and to assess risks apply, and the HSE has developed standards on managing stress at work (see pages 129–31 for more on stress).

- *Repetitive strain injury (RSI):* The Display Screen Equipment Regulations cover using VDUs, and the Management of Health and Safety at Work Regulations cover the need to assess risks (including RSI).

- *Noise:* If you are exposed to more than 80 decibels (dB) at work, your employer should be reducing the noise levels or at least giving you protection – the Noise at Work Regulations cover the issue.

- *Asbestos:* Exposure to asbestos kills more people than any other work-related hazard. The Control of Asbestos Regulations 2012 set out your employer's duties.

- *Temperature:* Minimum legal temperatures are set out in the Workplace (Health, Safety and Welfare) Regulations, but regarding maximum temperatures there is guidance only.

- *Asthma:* Workplace exposure to chemicals that cause asthma is covered by the Control of Substances Hazardous to Health (COSHH) Regulations, and the HSE has appended an Approved Code of Practice on asthma itself to the COSHH Regulations.

There are also specific requirements relating to the provision of first aid facilities and to the reporting of accidents at work or the occurrence of serious illnesses at work. For more details, contact your union or the HSE (address in Chapter 9).

If you work in a unionized workplace, it is likely that the union will have made a number of agreements on health and safety issues over and above the statutory minimum. These might include issues such as lifting heavy weights or the temperature in your workplace.

If you believe that you are being put into a dangerous situation at work and there is a 'dangerous and imminent risk' to you or fellow workers, you have the right to stop work and leave the area. If your employer disciplines you, you can apply for compensation or reinstatement if you are sacked. Before walking off the job you should, unless there really is no time, raise your concerns first with your manager and/or safety representative or union representative.

If the worst happens

Despite all the regulations, the work of the HSE and union action, 2 million people are injured at work every year and many more suffer a work-related illness. This is what you should do if you are injured or made ill by your work.

Firstly, report it to your line manager and/or safety representative. Get him or her to record it in the accident book. If you suffer some specified injuries and illnesses, your employer must tell the HSE. This does not necessarily trigger an inspection, but does allow the HSE to know what is happening in workplaces.

Secondly, or if you have problems with the first step, see your GP and explain how your work caused your injury or illness, and, if you are a member, tell your union. If appropriate, your GP or your employer may provide rehabilitation, such as physiotherapy, to get you back to fitness and back to work.

If your injury or illness causes you to lose wages, or causes pain and disability for more than a few weeks, you may be able to claim benefits from Jobcentre Plus, or compensation from your employer. If the injury was due to criminal violence, tell the police. You may be able to claim from the Ministry of Justice's Criminal Injuries Compensation Scheme.

Stress at work

Stress at work has been described as the new workplace epidemic. Every so often a spectacular case hits the headlines when someone wins a substantial award as compensation for suffering stress at work. But such cases are relatively rare; the more common reality is that workers are suffering in silence as stress levels rise each year. Many factors can add to stress levels. Long hours, exposure to noise, a heavy workload, little or no control over the pace of work, and poor management are just some of the common contributory factors.

If you do feel that workplace stress is damaging your health, speak to someone about it. It can be your line manager, a steward or, if you have one, a workplace human resources officer, but if you continue working in that environment it is likely to make you even more ill.

If you are suffering from a stress-related illness such as depression and anxiety, remember that the worst thing you can do is nothing. Make sure that you speak to your doctor. There are treatments available that can help people recover from a stress-related illness.

While at present it isn't possible to bring a claim of 'stress' in an employment tribunal, stress at work which isn't addressed is likely to get worse and even interfere with your normal day-to-day activities. In severe cases workers, supported by unions, have been able to seek compensation from their employer.

The priority should be to prevent cases of stress occurring. The first step is to try to identify the factors that are causing you to be stressed, as some causes are covered by regulations.

If long hours are the cause, you should check whether you are working longer than the Working Time Regulations allow (see Chapter 3). If noise levels are a problem, you should talk to your safety representative. Your hearing may also be in danger, and you should take urgent action.

If the real cause of your stress is your heavy workload, you should talk to your manager to see if he or she can take steps to relieve the burden. Many managers have little idea how long tasks they set can take. You should make sure they do. If they are not prepared to take the issue seriously and try to work through with you what needs to be done, you should ask them directly to take specific action to reduce your stress level. You are always best advised to put this in writing, and take notes of any discussion or write it up as soon as possible afterwards.

If your manager still refuses to deal with your problem, you should consider a formal grievance procedure if your employer has one (see pages 144–46 for more about grievance procedures).

If your stress gets to the point where it is making you ill or you really feel you cannot cope, you should go to see your GP and explain the problem. He or she will probably be willing to sign you off sick for a period of time. This may well bring the issue to a head. One can hope that this will persuade your employer that there is a serious problem and that something needs to be done about it. On the other hand, they may take action against you for absenteeism or 'under-performance' or for some other symptom of your stress.

If your employer takes action against you or continues to ignore your problem, you may have the basis of a court case, and you should seek advice. Your case might be that your employer is in breach of the implied duty in the contract of employment to provide a healthy and safe working environment for you. If you are stressed and tired, you are likely to be a hazard to yourself and other workers.

If you are dismissed, or feel that you simply cannot take any more and walk out, you may be able to claim constructive dismissal on the grounds that the situation made it impossible for you to continue working (see Chapter 7 for more about constructive dismissal). It is, however, hard to win constructive dismissal cases. You will almost certainly need to be able to show that you did everything possible to resolve the issue, including using any internal formal procedures, before you left your job.

Tackling the causes

There is no easy individual solution to workplace stress other than to tackle its causes. Research shows that it is not just the amount of work you have to do that leads to stress, but how much control you have over the pace of your work. Anything that gives you more control over how you work will help reduce stress levels.

This is an area where unions can usually achieve more than workers acting on their own. It is likely that other workers are also suffering. A union can present a joint case and approach the employer without any need for you to be personally involved – which would only be likely to add to your stress levels.

Macho-management is often a cause of stress. A workplace where a union has helped foster a spirit of partnership is far less likely to rely on top-down management. Giving employees more control over their own workloads reduces pressure and stress, and usually leads to people working more effectively.

Never forget that stress is avoidable, and the HSE have produced detailed guidance for employers on how to tackle it. These are contained in their Management Standards. Tackling stress does, however, require a long-term commitment from management and an acceptance, from the top, that things must change.

Other problems at work

Bullying

A TUC poll discovered that nearly a third of working people in Britain have been bullied at work. It can be a difficult issue to deal with, but if you are being bullied at work, by your employer, a line manager or a fellow worker, do not suffer in silence.

The basic legal protection you have against bullying, as with stress, is the implied duty in your contract of employment of your employer to protect you from any actions in the workplace that cause you ill health or put your safety at risk. This includes action taken by other workers.

Serious bullying can clearly cause you ill health or put your safety at risk, but less serious bullying should also be unacceptable, as it can often grow into more substantial bullying if left unchecked. If your workplace has a grievance procedure you should use this. If it does not, you should make a formal complaint in writing to your line manager. If he or she is the bully, go above his or her head, or go to your personnel or human resources department if there is one. If you are being bullied you should keep a diary of all the incidents, the effect they have on you and anything that you do to raise the issue. This will provide the evidence you need, especially if you can produce other witnesses.

If none of this works, you may be able to pursue a claim in court, using similar arguments to those for a stress case that your employer has failed to provide a safe and healthy working environment.

If the bullying involves an element of discrimination or harassment related to a 'protected characteristic', the law is clearer and you can probably make a complaint to an employment tribunal (see Chapter 6).

Drink and drugs

Alcohol and drug misuse can cause a range of problems at work. At one end is the genuine concern that people involved in dangerous or potentially dangerous activities such as driving a train, flying a plane or using dangerous machinery are not under the influence of any intoxicating substance. At the other end is an invasion of individual privacy. What you do in your spare time, as long as it has no effect on your ability to do your job, should not generally be of concern to your employer. If you are having problems with drink or drugs, you should seek specialist help. Some suggestions are given in Chapter 9.

While drugs throw up immediate problems because of their illegality, it is probably true to say that use of alcohol causes more work-related problems. But both can be a real hazard in the workplace, not just to you, but to your colleagues as well.

Although many people can function perfectly well at their jobs after a glass of wine or beer with their lunch, it is not unreasonable for employers to expect their staff to be clear-headed while at work. On the other hand, they should also realize that stress and other work-related problems can be the prime cause of drink and drug dependency.

Alcohol misuse

Sensible employers will have up-to-date policies for dealing with drink problems. About the worst way of dealing with alcoholism is ignoring it until it is too late. But it is easy for well-meaning colleagues, and even management, to carry on as normal until a drink problem deteriorates to the point where the only option is dismissal owing to chronic bad health, unreliability or other symptoms of alcohol dependency.

Many still see alcohol misuse as a personal failing – behaviour that shows a lack of moral fibre. In fact, it is often the diligent, conscientious worker who can no longer cope who misuses alcohol.

You will probably know if you have a problem with alcohol. This is a book about your rights at work and you should look elsewhere for advice on sensible drinking, but your employer would almost certainly have a good case for dismissing you for gross misconduct if you were routinely drunk or drinking at work, as long as the rules were applied fairly and uniformly across the workforce.

If your job involves protecting the safety of others – for example, driving a bus, train or plane – drinking will be strictly prohibited in your contract of employment, not just during working hours, but also for a set period before you begin each period of work, as alcohol remains in the body for some time after drinking. If your contract of employment prohibits alcohol, under the Health and Safety Act you are entitled to a copy of your employer's policy on alcohol in the workplace. If your employer intends to introduce such a policy, they are required to consult 'in good time' with their workforce, or union representatives, on the implications of the policy and how staff will be expected to comply with it.

However, automatic dismissal is not necessarily the best approach. A better way is for both you and your employer to recognize that you have a drink problem. In return for you seeking treatment or help in giving up or cutting down to sensible levels of social drinking, your employer should be prepared to provide support and some understanding that such problems cannot be solved overnight.

Ideally there should be ways of recognizing and dealing with a drink problem before it causes a breakdown in the employment relationship or leads you to do something that in itself would be likely to result in disciplinary action. If you believe that you are misusing alcohol, you should seek help before it causes problems with your employer. If you let the problem get worse, it will start to affect you at work.

Some companies have an occupational doctor or nurse, or a welfare officer, who would be able to provide confidential help.

If you are in a union, it may be able to help. Otherwise, you should seek assistance from your GP or from an organizations such as Alcohol Concern (see Chapter 9). They will try to establish why you are drinking too much. Work-related stress or other problems can be a factor that leads to drink problems. As we have seen earlier in this chapter, employers do have a duty of care and should not subject their staff to excess stress. This is one reason why they should not automatically deal with drink-related problems as a disciplinary matter. Poor employment practices may have triggered the problem in the first place.

Drug misuse

Many of the problems associated with the misuse of drugs at work are similar to those associated with the misuse of alcohol, and the ways in which you can tackle the problem are also similar. However, the most obvious *difference* is that alcohol is legal, while most recreational drugs are not. Your employer is perfectly within their rights to call the police if you are caught in possession of illegal drugs at work. You could be both prosecuted and dismissed for gross misconduct.

Some employers now use random testing in the workplace to help them to identify drug misuse. This is something of a legal grey area.

If you have worked for more than two years, it might well constitute unfair dismissal if you were sacked simply for refusing to provide a sample for a drugs test, unless you are bound by contractual agreement to do so and you are working in a safety-critical job. The right to privacy in the Human Rights Act may also give you some protection from your first day at work. As we said in Chapter 1, you can refuse to provide a drugs sample at a job interview but there is nothing to stop your potential employer rejecting you for the job if you do.

As with alcohol, you should ask for a copy of your employer's policy on drugs in the workplace. Depending on the method the employer uses to hold the results of your test, the employer may need to comply with the Data Protection Act. You are entitled to medical privacy, so make enquiries of your employer about the security of such information in the processes used by the employer and their testing laboratory services. If you are unsure about the methods being used by your employer, contact your union, your local HSE office or one of the alcohol and/or drugs advice agencies listed in Chapter 9.

Another tricky area is whether your employer can take action against you at work if you are prosecuted or cautioned for a drugs offence committed outside work and when there is no argument that drug-taking has affected your ability to do your job. Whether your employer, the government or unions like it or not, very many employees do take illegal recreational drugs. Whether you can claim unfair dismissal will depend on a number of factors if you are sacked as a result of a drugs offence outside work. An important one will be the nature of the job you do, and whether your offence will impact on your employer's reputation. To take an extreme example, if your job is promoting an 'anti-drugs' message, it would be hard to claim unfair dismissal if you are sacked for using drugs. If you are carrying out a routine job you may have a better chance. You will need to seek advice.

If you are using prescribed drugs at work that could, if misused, be dangerous, you may want to consider letting your employer know, though you are under no obligation to do this.

Organizations that can give advice on drugs are listed in Chapter 9.

Smoking

There can be no doubt that smoking is bad not just for your own health but for anyone who has to breathe your smoke. But those who smoke are usually addicted to smoking and find it difficult to go for long periods without a cigarette. Non-smokers, on the other hand, often find it objectionable as well as potentially hazardous to their health.

That is why smoking in workplaces and all public places has been banned since July 2007 in all the UK countries, with a small number of exemptions. However, tensions can remain over e-cigarettes, smoking outside and smoking breaks. Good employers have followed up the ban, providing help to staff who want to give up.

Contractual problems

Your contract of employment sets out the terms under which you are employed. Your employer cannot make changes to your contract unless you agree to them, and otherwise only if the contract says that your employer can make changes.

Good employers will seek your consent to any changes. If you refuse but accept them in practice by working to the new terms or conditions, the law may find that you have accepted the new terms and you could lose the right to object. So, if your employer tells you that you must now work an extra half-hour a day, you should tell your employer that you do not agree to the change and continue to leave work at your original time.

Terms implied by 'custom and practice' are specific to an employer or kind of work. They are not written down and relate to arrangements that have never been clearly agreed but over time have become part of the contract. For example, you might get a Christmas bonus every year, or the business might close early on particular days. If a company practice has become a part of your contract then your employer must stick to it, and cannot normally change it without your agreement.

Changes to your contract of employment may be made through an agreement between your employer and a recognized union (see Chapter 1). This may affect you even if you are not a member of the union if the union's agreement covers all workers in the workplace, or all workers on your grade.

If your employer wants to change the terms of your contract, they must give you a statement setting out the new conditions and asking you to accept them. If you do not agree and the change is implemented in any case, you can ask a civil court to rule that the employer is in breach of contract and sue for restoration of the original terms or damages. You cannot go to an employment tribunal for breach of contract claims unless you have been dismissed, or have left your job, as a result (see Chapter 8).

You are only likely to succeed in a claim if the change has fundamentally altered the contract. Examples where the courts would be likely to rule in your favour include reducing your wages, not paying you on time or failing to pay you at all. An example of a change where you would probably lose any claim would be if you were asked to move to a new type of computer. This would not normally constitute a fundamental change.

If you believe that the change is so fundamental that it makes it impossible for you to continue working, you can resign and claim constructive dismissal, although this is always risky (see Chapter 7).

If your employer gives you notice that they intend to change your contract, the law will see this as terminating your current contract and offering you a new one. This means that if you do not want to work under the new terms you may be able to claim unfair dismissal. A tribunal is unlikely, however, to find for you unless the changes are pretty radical (see Chapter 7).

When a breach of contract arises because your employer has unlawfully deducted sums from your salary, such as allowances, bonuses and shift premiums, that you were entitled to receive under your contract (or that were set out in a collective agreement that forms part of your contract), you can bring what's called an unlawful deduction from wages claim in an employment tribunal during your employment – without having to resign or be dismissed.

A move too far?

Mr Aslam worked for a bank in Leeds on a low salary. His contract contained a clear mobility clause that stated that he could be transferred to any of the bank's workplaces in the UK. Mr Aslam was told to move to the bank's Birmingham branch without notice, but he refused on both financial and personal grounds (he was offered no relocation expenses, and his wife had just suffered a miscarriage). The bank asserted that it had a clear right to insist on the transfer under the express mobility clause of Mr Aslam's contract. He resigned, claimed constructive dismissal and won.

The employer argued that they had simply invoked an explicit clause of the contract, but this was rejected. The EAT ruled that employers still have to meet the implied terms in any contract, and in particular when dealing with mobility clauses: reasonable notice must be given before exercising the power to transfer an employee; and a mobility clause must be operated in such a way as to make it feasible (an employee should not be required to do something that is, in practice, impossible). Also, a mobility clause is subject to a general duty not to behave in a way likely to destroy mutual trust and confidence between employer and employee.

In the same way that an employer is not entitled to apply a rule in any way they want, they are similarly not entitled to insist on a contractual right in any way they want. In both cases there is a duty of reasonableness.

Disciplinary procedures

If you get into trouble at work, or your employer thinks that you are not working effectively, your employer may decide to start a formal disciplinary procedure. Unless you are guilty of serious misconduct or your employer is acting unfairly, it is likely that this first stage of the procedure will end with you being given a verbal warning. Responsible employers will view a first stage as an opportunity to encourage you to improve your performance rather than punish you.

Acas (Advisory, Conciliation and Arbitration Service) has produced a Code of Practice on Disciplinary and Grievance Procedures, which all reasonable employers should follow, along with any additional internal procedures or rules that may apply to the workplace (see **www.acas.org.uk**). Workplace disciplinary and grievance procedures may be set out in your contract of employment or in a staff handbook or statement of employment particulars. If not, you can ask a human resources colleague, if you have one; otherwise you should ask a manager or someone more senior than you. In the public sector and larger private companies, disciplinary and grievance procedures are almost always available. A tribunal will accept a less formal procedure in a small company as fair, but will still expect it to allow you to give your point of view and follow some basic principles as set out in the Acas Code of Practice on Disciplinary and Grievance Procedures (see also Chapter 8).

The disciplinary procedure must be set out in writing, and you should receive a copy of it, or at least be told where you can get a copy, when you start work. Normally, a disciplinary procedure will have a number of stages of increasing seriousness, but your employer can dismiss you on the spot if you are guilty of a serious offence (known as 'gross misconduct') or suspend you from work on full pay while an investigation is carried out. Examples of gross misconduct offences are often contained in your contract of employment or the disciplinary procedure itself. They are likely to include offences such as assault, theft and workplace drug abuse.

If you are not accused of gross misconduct the first stage is likely to be a verbal warning. Your manager or another senior member of staff will call you in and tell you that you must improve your performance, or not continue to do something wrong. You could, for example, be told that you must stop being late for work. The warning is usually lifted if your behaviour or performance improves. The employer should tell you that the warning is formal and is the first part of the disciplinary procedure.

The next stage, if you do not improve your performance or behaviour, is likely to be a written warning. If the offence is regarded as more serious, your employer may go straight to this stage without giving a verbal warning. However, before issuing you with a written warning your employer should invite you to a meeting to discuss the matter. At the meeting you should be given the opportunity to ask questions, call witnesses and put forward your version of events. You have a right to be accompanied at the meeting by a work colleague or a trade union representative, if you have one. After the meeting your employer should write to you with the decision and whether a written warning will be issued and recorded on your personnel file. Generally, the written warning will be removed from your file after a year.

There may be provision for a final written warning, which can be the last stage before dismissal. This warning must tell you that dismissal is a possibility and also tell you about any appeal procedure. Again, if a final warning is given, it is likely that the warning will be kept on your file for at least a year.

You have a legal right to be accompanied by a trade union representative or official, or a workplace colleague (see below). You are strongly advised to exercise that right and to choose somebody who has had past experience of handling disciplinary hearings in your workplace. If you, or your chosen representative, cannot attend at the time or date given, you have a legal right to ask for a postponement of up to five days, and for a rearranged hearing at a different time and date. Your employer should send you a statement setting out what you have done, or failed to do, that might result in disciplinary action or dismissal.

At the hearing, your employer will explain why you have been asked to attend. You or your representative will then be invited to make an opening statement so that you can explain your behaviour or refute the charge, depending on the circumstances. You are allowed to call witnesses in your support. But you should make sure that they understand why they are being called and what they are being asked to do. You should not ask anyone to do anything but tell the truth, but it is perfectly legitimate to talk through with your witnesses what they will say to make sure it is helpful. You can be sure that your employer is doing the same with the witnesses they are likely to call. It is important to prepare your case carefully and be sure of all your facts. You should do this with the person who will be accompanying you. Think through what is likely to be said against you and how best you can respond to it. For example, it may be better to present your case in a way that suggests your accuser has made an honest mistake (if this is consistent with the facts).

A formal disciplinary hearing, particularly in a larger company, is likely to be before more than a single manager. It could, for example, be dealt with by a senior manager, the personnel or human resources manager and your line manager or supervisor.

After the hearing, your employer will let you know, probably both verbally and in writing, what has been decided. This could be dismissal, with appropriate notice or, if agreed by you or provided for in your contract, payment in lieu of notice. Dismissal decisions should only be taken by senior managers. Other penalties might be a transfer, suspension with or without pay, demotion or loss of increment, but only if such penalties are allowed for in your contract or agreed by you.

The written notification of the penalty should include the reasons for it. If you are dismissed and have been employed by your employer continuously for more than two years, you have a statutory right to written reasons for dismissal (see Chapter 7).

Your employer must also inform you of your right of appeal. You will probably have to lodge your appeal within a certain, probably short, period of time, often five working days. The appeal should be heard by someone more senior than you who has not previously been involved in the disciplinary procedure. In a small business this may not be possible. Again, you have a right to be accompanied by your union representative or by a colleague. It is likely that you or your representative will be invited to open the proceedings by explaining why you are appealing against the decision to discipline or dismiss you. Both you and your representative may ask questions of your employer's witnesses, and you should get a verbal decision, followed by a written decision, on the same day or as soon as possible after this.

Failure by your employer to follow the Acas Code of Practice could count against them if you make a subsequent claim at an employment tribunal and succeed. A tribunal can increase the amount of compensation you are awarded. If you fail to attend a hearing, unless it is for good reason, your compensation can be reduced even if the tribunal finds the dismissal to have been unfair (see Chapter 8).

It may be that your employer has more than one complaint about you. If so, each should be treated as a separate issue, particularly when establishing whether it is justified or not. However, if it comes to deciding a penalty for multiple offences it is legitimate for your employer to consider them together.

In practice, many employers will put complaints together and deal with them in one procedure and at one hearing. If this is the case, you should insist that each offence be dealt with individually. You should not allow your employer simply to create a general impression of your alleged failures as a substitute for a proper investigation of the facts in each case.

A criminal prosecution outside the workplace should not automatically trigger the workplace disciplinary procedure, though when this might occur may be specified in your contract. If, for example, you are prosecuted and found guilty of an offence against children and you are employed in a job that involves working with children, you must expect a disciplinary procedure at work.

A criminal prosecution for an offence committed in the workplace is likely to trigger dismissal for gross misconduct, depending on the nature of the offence. Your employer, however, should not rely on an outside process. They should still conduct their own investigation regardless of the criminal prosecution. You may be suspended pending the criminal investigation. This should be on full pay until the case is decided, unless your contract provides otherwise.

A fight to the finish?

Jason Green was involved in an argument with his supervisor. During the argument the supervisor questioned the fidelity of Jason's wife, and Jason punched the supervisor. He was sacked. The employer argued that this was an inevitable consequence of striking a superior. But Jason claimed unfair dismissal, and won.

The tribunal did not agree with the employer that dismissal was the inevitable consequence of Jason's action. The degree of provocation should be looked at, and Jason had acted under severe provocation.

However, this should not be taken as a green light to hit your boss! There are very few cases where anyone has won an unfair dismissal case after striking a manager.

Grievance procedures

Do not confuse these with disciplinary procedures, which are used where your employer believes that you have done something wrong or are not performing well. Grievance procedures are for use where *you* have a grievance or a complaint about something that is happening at work. In other words, disciplinary procedures are when your employer thinks you are doing something wrong. Grievance procedures are for when you think *you* are the victim.

There is currently a legal requirement for your employer to have a grievance procedure. You must be given information about it when you start work. This can be either in your staff handbook or provided with your contract or statement of written particulars of employment. You must use it before taking a tribunal case.

You will probably not be entitled to trigger a grievance procedure for a relatively trivial issue, such as being mildly irritated by a colleague's habit of chewing gum all day. But you should be free to raise any more serious matter. This may be a complaint about something your employer or manager is doing or not doing, or a complaint about the conduct of another member of staff that you believe your employer should stop. Issues that you should be able to raise at a grievance procedure include bullying, impossible deadlines, sexual, racial or any other kind of harassment, or seriously uncomfortable working conditions.

Some grievances indicate the development of serious general workplace issues, such as those relating to health and safety or discrimination. Others may only be serious for you. In either case, good employers will take any grievance seriously unless investigation confirms them as minor matters.

Details will differ from workplace to workplace, but you will usually need to put your grievance in writing to your immediate supervisor or line manager to trigger the procedure. An effort may be made at this stage by your employer to resolve the matter more informally; indeed, you may have lodged the grievance as a way of underlining its seriousness but with the aim of settling the issues informally. If you think this is a genuine effort then it may be appropriate to cooperate, but if you think it is simply a time-wasting dodge or a way of excluding your representative, insist on a formal hearing.

If you have a trade union representative he or she will be able to help and advise you about the best way of bringing a successful grievance procedure. He or she will also be able to accompany you at the formal hearing, as you have the same representation rights as at a disciplinary hearing (see below for more details).

The formal grievance hearing will probably take place before one or more senior managers, probably with someone from your personnel or human resources department. It will be up to you to make your case. Procedures vary from organization to organization, but you are allowed to present written evidence in support of your case and to call witnesses. If, for example, you were complaining about the stress caused by a heavy workload, a letter from your doctor would help. If you are complaining about harassment, if there are any witnesses you should aim to call them or present written statements from them. You should receive the result of the hearing as soon as possible, in writing. Good practice would be to let you have the written ruling within five working days.

If you are not happy with the outcome, you should be able to raise it again with a more senior manager at an appeal stage. Another shorter hearing may well take place, depending on the nature of the grievance. Again, you have the right to be accompanied.

If you still do not get a satisfactory response, there may be provision (in a larger company) for a further full grievance hearing, involving the most senior manager in the organization or plant, and even a further appeal stage beyond that. Again, in the final hearing and at the appeal, depending on the nature of the grievance, you have the right to be accompanied.

Once you have exhausted your employer's procedures and you are still not satisfied, you may be able to go to an employment tribunal or the civil courts. You would normally have to show that your employer had denied you your legal rights or was in breach of your contract of employment, including the implied duties discussed earlier in this chapter. If you cannot show this, there is little more that you can do, unless you are in a unionized workplace and your union is able to take the matter up as being one of more general concern to all the staff.

The right to be accompanied

All workers have the right, on making a reasonable request, to be accompanied at a disciplinary or grievance hearing. This right applies to all workers, not only to employees, so it does not matter whether or not you have a contract of employment with your employer or hiring company. You have the right to be accompanied by a trade union officer or representative, or a fellow worker (often referred to as a 'companion'). You do not have the right, except in very limited circumstances, to bring in a lawyer or other adviser. Union officers and representatives will have been trained and accredited to accompany workers. They are likely to bring valuable experience to any formal proceedings. They can accompany you even if the union is not 'recognized'.

If a union is recognized by your employer (see Chapter 1), it is very likely that there will be an agreed disciplinary and grievance procedure and the union will have full representation rights in relation to its members. This is one of the normal benefits of union recognition, and in some workplaces there are employer–union agreements on disciplinary and grievance issues even where there are no negotiations on pay and conditions.

The legal right to be accompanied at a disciplinary hearing is triggered when you make a 'reasonable request'. What is reasonable will depend on the individual circumstances, but if you ask to be accompanied by your chosen companion and give your employer enough information and time to allow them to deal with the practicalities of their attendance at the hearing then your request is likely to be considered 'reasonable'.

It is important to exercise your right to be accompanied where the hearing could result in a formal warning, confirmation of a previous formal warning or some other action such as suspension, demotion or dismissal. It is, therefore, widely drawn and it is hard to see how your representative could be excluded from any formal hearing. You may change your mind about who you would like to accompany you at a meeting. You should notify your employer of any change if you do. If your chosen companion isn't available your employer must postpone the hearing to a time proposed by you as long as the alternative time is reasonable and not more than five working days after the date originally proposed.

The right to be accompanied does not apply to a more informal conversation with your manager about your conduct, though if you think a discussion that starts out informally has become formal you should say so and ask for it to be resumed with your representative present and under proper procedures. On the other hand, it may be best to keep things informal, as this prevents formal action being taken against you.

With grievance hearings, the right to be accompanied only applies if your complaint concerns a legal duty owed to you by your employer, for example your employer's obligation to ensure that you are not bullied or harassed. In practice it should be possible to argue that any likely grievance may have a bearing on a legal duty, and it is unlikely that any but the most grudging or anti-union employer will try to differentiate between legal and non-legal grievances, although they may screen complaints that they consider to be trivial.

If your employer tries to prevent you from exercising your right to be accompanied or prevents your chosen companion from attending you can make a complaint to an employment tribunal. You may wish to talk to your union representative or an advice agency before starting any claim.

Chapter Six
Discrimination

The principles behind the law on discrimination are easy to state. In practice, however, this is a complicated area of law.

Even though some anti-discrimination law has been on the statute books for more than 30 years, there is still some way to go. Women, on average, earn less than men. Despite some progress, people in positions of authority at the top of organizations, and even in middle management and supervisory roles, are more likely to be white and male.

It is more than 20 years since disability discrimination laws were first introduced, yet disabled people face considerable barriers to getting good jobs.

Laws protecting against discrimination on the basis of age, sexual orientation and religion or belief are more recent. Trade unions have long campaigned for UK equality laws to be streamlined and consolidated. The Equality Act 2010 was a significant achievement in that it brought together nine separate pieces of discrimination law into a single Act and streamlined many of the legal definitions applying to the different equality groups.

The Equality Act 2010

Protected characteristics

You have the right not to be discriminated against at work because of your age, disability, gender reassignment, marriage or civil partnership status, pregnancy or maternity, race, religion or belief, sex and sexual orientation. The law refers to these categories or groups as 'protected characteristics'. The Equality Act ('the Act') also provides for equal pay between men and women. This chapter outlines your basic rights, but this is one of the most complex areas of employment law. If you run into problems you should always consult your union representative or a legal or other specialist adviser.

The good news is that discrimination laws apply to almost everyone at work. They cover you when you apply for a job and from the first day of your job. It does not matter whether you are an employee, a worker, self-employed or a trainee.

If the discrimination happens while you are at work or while you are working for your employer, your employer is liable, even if it is not the employer personally who is discriminating against you.

If you think you have been discriminated against unlawfully, you can take a case to an employment tribunal, but you must do this within three months of the incident you are complaining about. You might be awarded compensation and damages. This award can include an element of compensation to cover injury to your feelings. There is no upper limit on the amount that can be awarded in discrimination claims, and some large awards have hit the headlines. However, these large awards are the exception, not the rule.

Age

The age provisions of the Act protect all workers from discrimination because of age – not just older workers. For example, if you've been denied a promotion because you are 'too young' or refused access to development training because you don't have as many years of employment ahead of you as younger colleagues, you may have a claim. You will also be protected from discrimination based on your perceived age – for example, if someone says you look too young or too old for a job.

Traditionally, there have been many age-based rules in the workplace; however, age discrimination protection is different from the other laws because it allows employers to justify direct discrimination if they can show that it is a proportionate way of them achieving a legitimate business goal. For example, an employer may decide that for health and safety reasons they do not want to employ someone in a job that involves operating dangerous machinery because of the person's age. The employer would have to make sure, though, that their decision was based on an objective assessment of the actual risk, rather than just being based on stereotypical assumptions about younger or older workers.

The law also specifically allows some age-related policies or practices. For example, service-related pay and benefits that are based on service up to five years are allowed. So are age-based rates of pay that mirror the national minimum wage, the age-based bands in the statutory redundancy pay scheme, and some age-related rules and benefits in occupational pension schemes.

Employers can no longer force you to retire on your 65th birthday unless they can objectively justify their actions. You can now challenge your employer's decision to compulsorily retire you once you have reached a certain age as age discrimination and unfair dismissal. You can still voluntarily retire if you wish and draw any occupational pension you are entitled to; normally this is available from age 55 onwards.

Disability

The Equality Act gives disabled workers protection against discrimination at work. It prohibits discrimination against disabled job applicants, employees and contractors. It applies to recruitment, promotion, employee benefits, disciplinary proceedings, dismissal, harassment and victimization.

To be protected you must be a 'disabled' person as defined by the Act. This means you must have a physical or mental impairment and the impairment must have a substantial and long-term adverse effect on your ability to carry out normal day-to-day activities. There is no prescribed list of normal day-to-day activities that must be affected by the mental or physical impairment. Instead, it will be for you to show that your normal day-to-day activities are adversely affected.

The impairment or condition must be long-term, which is defined as lasting, or expected to last, at least 12 months or for the rest of the person's life.

A wide range of conditions are covered, for example:

- conditions that may only have a slight effect on day-to-day activities, but that are expected to become substantial, for example arthritis;

- conditions that meet the definition of disability from the point of diagnosis, such as cancer, multiple sclerosis and HIV infection;

- conditions that would have a serious effect if not controlled by medication, eg severe depression, or by aids such as artificial limbs;

- conditions that fluctuate such as ME; and

- severe disfigurements.

The Act also covers impairments caused by mental health issues, such as depression and anxiety, learning difficulties and autism.

The law on disability discrimination is complicated, and you should not embark on a case without taking specialist advice. You can take a case to an employment tribunal, and claims have to be made within three months of the act (or last act) of discrimination you are complaining about. The tribunal can award compensation, including for injury to feelings. There is currently no upper limit on compensation. The tribunal may also recommend that the employer make adjustments in the workplace.

Gender reassignment

A person has the protected characteristic of 'gender reassignment' if he or she is proposing to undergo, is undergoing or has undergone a process of gender reassignment. There is no need for this process to be a medical procedure. So someone who is born physically female, starts to live as a man and finds that he successfully passes as a man and does not wish to go through a medical procedure for gender reassignment would be protected under the Act.

Marriage and civil partnership

To have the protected characteristic of marriage or civil partnership you must be either married or a civil partner. You are not protected if you live with your partner, are single or are engaged to be married (or a civil partner), nor are you protected if you have been widowed or divorced.

Pregnancy and maternity

The Act protects a woman against unfavourable treatment because:

- she is pregnant;
- she has an illness relating to her pregnancy;
- she is on compulsory maternity leave;
- she is about to take, is taking or has taken ordinary or additional maternity leave.

Race

Under the Equality Act 'race' means protection from discrimination because of colour, nationality, or ethnic or national origin. It also protects you if you are discriminated against because someone perceives you as belonging to a particular racial group or if you associate with someone of a different racial group – for example, if you are married to someone of a different ethnic background – and you are harassed at work because of this relationship.

Religion or belief

The Act protects against discrimination because of religion or belief or because of a lack of religion or belief. The terms 'religion' and 'belief' are not defined in the Act, so it will ultimately be for a tribunal to decide what qualifies as a religion or belief for the purposes of protection from discrimination. But generally speaking a belief or religion must:

- be genuinely held;
- be a belief about a weighty and substantial aspect of human life and behaviour;
- have a certain level of cogency, seriousness, cohesion and importance;
- be worthy of respect in a democratic society;
- be a belief and not just an opinion or viewpoint;
- be compatible with human dignity and not conflict with the rights of other people.

Courts and tribunals will consider things such as whether or not there is collective worship or a clear system of beliefs that profoundly affects and determines how you live your life. In addition to well-recognized religions, other beliefs such as paganism are covered, as are atheism and agnosticism.

There are specific exceptions within the law that mean that religious or faith-based organizations can require that you share their religious beliefs in order to be employed by them. However, these exceptions are not as wide as you might think, and they do not apply to all jobs within such organizations. For example, it may be lawful for a faith-based school recruiting a pastoral care teacher to require applicants to belong to the religion if the job involves giving spiritual guidance on a regular basis, but it would be difficult for the faith-based school to insist that its maths teacher or school receptionist share the same religious ethos.

Sex

The Equality Act protects you against discrimination because of your sex. It also specifically protects women from being treated unfavourably because they are pregnant or on maternity leave.

Because women are more likely to be carers and to work part-time the protection from sex discrimination often overlaps with other areas of employment law. For example, if a woman has a request for flexible working turned down, this could be indirect sex discrimination, as a refusal to allow flexible working practices will put more women than men at a disadvantage. Similarly, if you are a woman working part-time and you are being treated less favourably than full-timers you might have a sex discrimination claim as well as a claim under the Part-Time Worker Regulations.

It is also important to note that, if you are being paid less or receiving worse contractual terms and conditions than someone of the opposite sex who is doing similar work, this is covered by the equal pay provisions of the Equality Act, which are explained later in this chapter.

Sexual orientation

The Act protects against discrimination because of a person's sexual orientation towards:

- others of the same sex – lesbians and gay men;
- those of the opposite sex – heterosexuals;
- those of either sex – bisexual.

Prohibited conduct

The UK discrimination laws now share a common approach and similar definitions. The law generally prohibits certain kinds of actions, known as 'prohibited conduct'. These are direct discrimination, indirect discrimination, discrimination arising from disability and failure to make reasonable adjustments (applies to disability only), harassment and victimization. Discrimination occurs when you are subjected to treatment that is prohibited conduct because of a protected characteristic. In some cases, even if you do not have the particular protected characteristic you can claim discrimination, for example if you have been treated less favourably because others (wrongly) perceive that you have the characteristic or because you associate with someone else who has that characteristic.

Direct discrimination

People directly discriminate against you if, because of a protected characteristic, they treat you less favourably than they treat or would treat others. Examples of direct discrimination include offering a training opportunity or promotion to a male employee but not to a woman 'because she might go off and have a baby', or where a well-qualified black person applies for a job and is told it has gone, and then a white person applies and is offered an interview.

Generally, direct discrimination cannot be justified. For example, it won't help for an employer to try to defend their actions by arguing that they were not malicious or that they were 'only joking' and didn't intend to discriminate.

Nor will it matter that the person discriminating and the victim of discrimination share the same protected characteristic. For example, a female director who fails to offer a young woman an opportunity for promotion (that is, or would be, offered to a man) for fear she will 'start a family soon' will be directly discriminating against her because of sex.

Even if the opportunity for promotion is not actually offered to a man (because none are employed in that team), failing to offer a woman the chance for promotion because she might start a family would still be direct discrimination if the offer would have been made to a man.

While it is helpful to be able to identify an actual comparator it is not always essential; a comparator can be a real or hypothetical person as long as there is no material difference in their circumstances.

Even where employers don't realize they are discriminating, the unfavourable treatment is still unlawful.

Associative discrimination

The person who suffers less favourable treatment because of a protected characteristic needn't have that characteristic. A claim may be brought by someone who is treated less favourably than others because he or she 'associates' with someone else who has the protected characteristic. For example, a working mother who was treated less favourably by her employer because she needed time off to care for her disabled son successfully claimed disability discrimination.

It isn't possible to bring a claim of associative discrimination because of pregnancy and maternity or marriage and civil partnership. If you are unclear about whether you have suffered associative discrimination seek advice from your union or one of the agencies listed in Chapter 9.

Perception discrimination

Direct discrimination also covers discrimination because of perception, for example if a man is refused the opportunity for promotion because he is wrongly perceived to be gay. Perception discrimination does not apply to pregnancy and maternity or marriage and civil partnership.

Indirect discrimination

Indirect discrimination is a harder concept to pin down. It happens when an employer applies a 'provision, criterion or practice' that puts people who share a protected characteristic at a particular disadvantage when compared to others who do not. Employers may be able to avoid a ruling against them if they can show that the provision, criterion or practice was a proportionate way of them achieving a legitimate business goal. However, if there is an obvious, less discriminatory way of them achieving the same goal it will be hard for them to justify the provision, criterion or practice and it could be ruled unlawful.

The following examples show how indirect discrimination can happen:

- A bus company's recruitment literature says that its drivers must have a high level of fluency in English in order to drive a bus with a conductor. But it may be hard for it to justify the need for such strong language skills, as the conductor will be dealing with all the passengers. Therefore the requirement could be unlawful race discrimination because it puts people of different national or ethnic origins at a disadvantage. On the other hand, if the company was recruiting for a one-person bus and the driver had to collect fares and help passengers, the company could legitimately require higher standards of English.

- A shop decides to open seven days a week and draws up a roster that means some Sunday working for all employees. One worker is a devout Christian and objects to working on Sundays. The employer refuses to listen to her objections and insists that all employees must work on Sundays. She decides she has no choice but to resign. She may be able to successfully claim indirect religious discrimination, and her case would be strengthened by the fact that the employer did not consider any alternatives – for example, there may have been others within the workforce who wanted to work more Sundays and would have swapped shifts with her.

- A firm operates a 'last in, first out' (LIFO) redundancy policy. As older workers are likely to have longer service than younger workers, this policy is indirectly discriminatory against younger workers. It could therefore be unlawful, particularly if LIFO is the only criterion used to select people for redundancy. However, if it is one of a wide range of factors that are taken into consideration the employer may be justified in using it.

Indirect discrimination cases are very tricky. You have to show that people who share a protected characteristic have been put at a particular disadvantage and that the provision, criterion or practice in question also puts you at a disadvantage. It is then up to your employer to show that the provision, criterion or practice is a proportionate way of achieving a legitimate aim. If you work for a public sector employer, your employer is under an additional legal duty to prevent unlawful discrimination and promote equality of opportunity between groups who share protected characteristics and those who don't. This means that they should be monitoring and publishing information about workforce equality and assessing the impact of their policies on different groups. Further information about the public sector equality duty can be gained from the Equality and Human Rights Commission or from your union representative.

Discrimination arising from disability

The Act protects employees with disabilities who suffer discrimination not because of the disability itself but because of something arising in consequence of it. For example, if you have multiple sclerosis and it tends to 'flare up' periodically, giving rise to short-term absences from work, and you are dismissed because of your absences, you could claim discrimination arising from disability. It won't be possible to claim, however, unless your employer knows (or ought reasonably to know) about your impairment. While there is no obligation on you to tell your employer, choosing not to tell means that you will not be protected by the Act and your employer will not be obliged to make reasonable adjustments to remove any disadvantage that you face. Should you bring a claim, it would be open to your employer to show that the dismissal (or other treatment) was a proportionate way of fulfilling a legitimate aim.

Harassment

Discrimination laws protect you from harassment linked to protected characteristics. Harassment is defined as behaviour that has the purpose or effect of violating your dignity or creates an intimidating, hostile, degrading, humiliating or offensive environment for you. The person who is harassing you may claim that he or she was just joking or that it was just 'firm management', but you don't have to prove that the person intended to harass or upset you. If you make a legal claim, a tribunal will objectively assess what the effect of the person's behaviour was and will particularly consider your perception of it.

It is also not necessary for you to have the protected characteristic that the behaviour is linked to or for you to be the target of the behaviour. For example, if you overhear colleagues repeatedly telling racist jokes in the staff canteen you could bring a racial harassment claim if you could show it created an offensive environment for you.

If you are being harassed it isn't always necessary that you make it clear to the harasser that you find his or her behaviour offensive. A serious one-off incident may still be harassment even if you have not told your employer about it. Remember, your employer has a duty to protect you from such treatment, and they are liable if they do not take action to prevent it. Also tell your union representative or other adviser and keep evidence of the harasser's behaviour, perhaps in a diary, and try to get witnesses.

An insult to dignity

Mr English was the subject of homophobic mockery at his workplace. He claimed harassment under section 5 of the Employment Equality (Sexual Orientation) Regulations 2003, but the tribunal rejected his claim because he admitted that none of his work colleagues actually thought he was gay. The Court of Appeal overturned the employment appeal tribunal's decision, saying it did not matter whether he was gay or not. The calculated insult to his dignity, which depended not at all on his actual sexuality, and the consequently intolerable working environment were sufficient to bring his case. The incessant mockery created a degrading and hostile working environment, and it did so on grounds of sexual orientation.

Victimization

Victimization occurs when someone is treated unfavourably after complaining about or alleging discrimination or harassment. It includes actions taken against you after you have left employment, such as a refusal by your former employer to give you a reference. The law also protects you from victimization if you have helped someone else bring a complaint, for example if you gave evidence on behalf of a colleague in a discrimination case.

Pre-employment health questions

An employer is prohibited by law from asking about the health of a job applicant:

- before making an offer of work to the applicant; or
- before including the applicant in the pool from which the successful applicant will be chosen.

Asking a 'health question' includes, for example, whether you have a disability or whether you have a medical condition that the employer should know about. It also includes asking questions about previous sickness absence. There are, however, some exceptions – for instance, where it is necessary for the employer to establish whether you need a reasonable adjustment to be made so that you can participate fully in the recruitment process, or because the employer wants to take positive action to support under-represented groups in the workplace.

A breach of the ban on asking health questions does not, of itself, give rise to a claim in the employment tribunal, but if the employer relies on the information you give in order to refuse you the job their actions may constitute disability discrimination. If you have been asked questions about your health that you believe could be unlawful before being offered a job then you should contact the Equality and Human Rights Commission, who have responsibility for enforcing the ban.

Failure to make reasonable adjustments

An important protection for disabled workers is the duty to make reasonable adjustments. The idea of 'reasonable adjustments' is to remove obstacles that place the disabled person at a disadvantage. Examples could be altering premises, changing working hours, allowing time off for treatment, buying new equipment, supplying additional training or even just providing a reserved parking space. What is 'reasonable' depends on the individual case, but you have to take into account how effective the adjustment will be, the cost and the employer's resources. Clearly an employer cannot be expected to make adjustments unless they have been informed of your disability and needs.

You may be able to bring a tribunal case against your employer if you can show that your employer knew about your disability and failed to make reasonable adjustments to remove the obstacles you faced.

Exceptions to discrimination law

- *More favourable treatment of a disabled person:* It will not be direct discrimination to treat a disabled person more favourably than a non-disabled person.

- *Pregnancy and childbirth:* It will not be direct discrimination to give special treatment to a woman because of her pregnancy or childbirth.

- *Genuine occupational requirement:* This is a requirement for the job-holder to have a particular protected characteristic, which will apply to very few situations, for instance where there is a need for authenticity such as an actor being required to play a character who is a woman or who is black.

Positive action

The Act allows employers to do things in order to support and advance equality for employees who may be under-represented in the workplace, experience disadvantage or have different needs that relate to a protected characteristic. For example, an employer might set aside places on a training course for employees with a protected characteristic where participation from that group is ordinarily low. Employers can also use positive action when recruiting new staff. This covers a tie-break situation in which two candidates are as qualified as each other for the job; the employer may appoint the candidate with a protected characteristic that is under-represented in the workplace. However, this doesn't mean that you can expect to get a job just because you are a woman or because of your sexual orientation. Appointments should always be made on merit, and your employer cannot have a policy of automatically shortlisting women candidates – even if women are an under-represented group.

Equal pay

EU and UK laws give women and men in the same employment the right to equal pay. Under the equal pay provisions of the Equality Act a woman can claim equal pay with a man who is doing:

- 'like work' (that is, work that is the same or broadly similar); or
- 'work rated equivalent' under a job evaluation study; or
- 'work of equal value'.

If you are a woman making an equal pay claim you have to compare your pay with that of a man in 'equal work', whether the work is the same as or similar to that which you do, rated as equivalent to yours following job evaluation, or entirely different but of equal value to your work.

Your first step, therefore, is to find a suitable man, who will be known as the 'comparator'. He does not have to agree to this. This can be difficult, as particularly in workplaces where there tend to be individual salary packages rather than groups all doing the same job, it can be hard to find out how much other people earn. Acas provides guidance on asking employers for information in discrimination cases, which includes guidance on obtaining information in equal pay cases (see **www.acas.org.uk**). Not everyone can be a comparator. The law says that the comparator has to be 'in the same employment'. Clearly, anyone who works with you and has the same employer can be a comparator, but it can be stretched more widely than this. You can also choose a comparator who works 'at the same establishment' for an associated employer. If this is not possible, you can also look for a comparator at another workplace if the place of work meets two conditions. Firstly, it must belong to your employer (or to an associated employer). Secondly, people must be working on the same terms and conditions. In the public sector this can give quite a wide scope for comparison, but it can be tougher in the private sector, particularly in a small business.

How far you can look for a comparator is one of those complex areas of law where it is very hard to give general guidance. Many cases will depend on precisely this point, and different courts and tribunals have interpreted the law in different ways. Also, EU law lets you make wider comparisons than UK law. This is an area where it is crucial to get expert advice.

Once you have found your comparator there are three ways you can establish you are not getting equal pay.

The first is the most straightforward test. You have to show that your comparator is doing 'the same or broadly similar work'. This does not mean that you have to be doing identical jobs. They can count as broadly similar as long as any differences between them are not of 'practical importance'. A difference of 'practical importance' could include extra responsibility or additional duties.

The second way you can claim equal pay is by showing that your comparator is doing work that has been 'rated as equivalent under a job evaluation scheme'. This is the kind of scheme that employers often use to set their pay structures.

Normally, outside experts with experience of this work and a wide knowledge of how different organizations relate pay to different jobs will carry out the evaluation. They will look at all the different jobs and rate them by different criteria such as the responsibilities involved, the skills required and the knowledge needed. You will probably end up with scores of some kind for each job.

You cannot make your employer carry out a job evaluation exercise in order to make an equal pay claim. But if they have done one and accepted its results you can bring a claim using this as your evidence.

The job evaluation scheme must also meet certain tests. The court will need to know that it was thorough, with proper tools used to measure each job. It cannot just be a rough ranking of jobs drawn up on the back of an envelope.

The third way of claiming equal pay is by showing that your work is of equal value to that done by a man in the same employment, even though his job is different. In some ways you can think of this as a do-it-yourself job evaluation scheme. You have to show that your work is equal in value to that done by your comparator, using the same kind of headings such as effort, skill and decision making that a job evaluation study would use.

But claiming equal pay for work of equal value is more complicated than showing that you are doing 'like work' or work rated as equivalent under a job evaluation scheme. Again, you have to find your 'equal value' comparator. He must successfully meet the 'in the same employment' test requirements as a comparator who is doing the same job as you. But you can look much wider, as you need to find a man paid more than you but whose job has the same value even if it is completely different.

Successful 'equal value' comparisons have been made between:

- a female canteen worker and a male shipyard worker;
- female fish packers and a general labourer;
- nursery nurses and a waste technician and an architectural technician; and
- a speech therapist and a senior pharmacist and a senior clinical psychologist.

The tribunal procedure for claiming equal pay for work of equal value is more complicated than in other equal pay cases. You should not even think of taking an equal value case without seeking expert advice. You should also bear in mind that you can take an equal pay case to a tribunal only while you are still employed or within six months after the end of employment, unless certain exceptions apply, such as where your employer has deliberately concealed an important fact relating to your case. You will need expert advice in these circumstances.

If you can't find a man to compare yourself with, perhaps because there are no men employed in similar work, you may be able to claim direct sex discrimination if, for instance, you can show that your employer would have paid you more had you been a man.

Pay secrecy clauses

Pay secrecy clauses are usually found in your contract of employment. They aim to prevent you discussing your salary with colleagues. Under the Act these clauses are no longer enforceable, which means that an employer cannot claim that an employee who discusses his or her salary with others has breached his or her contract of employment. You can now discuss salary not just with your colleagues but with a trade union representative or official, or other adviser, as long as the purpose of the discussion is to find out whether there is any discriminatory difference in pay.

Part-time work

Part-time work is not defined in law. It is generally taken to mean any hours below the normal full-time hours where you work. Part-time workers have some protection in law against discrimination, both under the Equality Act and under regulations introduced in 2000, as we explain below.

Part-time workers – sex discrimination and equal pay

Most part-time workers are women, and discrimination against part-time workers can often be indirect sex discrimination (we explain earlier in this chapter how to spot indirect discrimination). Excluding part-time workers from pay-related benefits, or paying them lower hourly rates, can in some circumstances be indirect pay discrimination because of sex.

There have been some successful cases – but indirect discrimination is always more difficult to show than direct. You have to show that the employer is applying a 'provision, criterion or practice' that affects considerably more women than men.

For example, your employer might have a rule saying that only full-time workers can get contractual sick pay. If most of the men in your workplace work full-time and most of the women part-time, that could be indirect discrimination unless the employer can justify the rule. But your claim could fail, for example, if you work for an employer where there are no or very few men and most of the women employees are full-time. In a case like that, you could not show that more women than men are adversely affected by the employer's rule.

Other examples of possible indirect sex discrimination claims might be where:

- Your employer excludes part-time workers from benefits like private health insurance or a profit-related bonus scheme. If, where you work, most of the men work full-time and most of the women work part-time, more women than men would be excluded, so a claim might succeed.

● Full-time workers get extra annual leave after one year's service, while part-time workers have to work for two years before getting more holiday. Again, if most of the full-time workers are men and most of the part-time workers women, you could have a case of indirect sex discrimination.

Another way some women have successfully used the indirect discrimination provisions is by arguing that they should be able to come back to work after maternity leave on reduced hours. The argument is that more women than men find it difficult to work full-time, because more women than men are carers of young children.

Conversely fathers can face direct sex discrimination because of this cultural assumption that it should be women who work part-time. The recent *Pietzka v PWC* case highlights the view expressed by managers that working part-time would harm career prospects for men.

Although some cases have been won on the basis of the indirect discrimination provisions, others have not. There is a clear case for a change in the law to give stronger rights for working parents and carers, as this indirect discrimination route is very uncertain. You should not think of trying this route without first taking specialist advice. In the meantime, other rights for working parents and carers may help you (see Chapter 4).

Part-Time Workers (Prevention of Less Favourable Treatment) Regulations

These regulations should make it easier for part-time workers to claim equality with full-time workers without having to enter the minefield of indirect sex discrimination. The regulations do not give you the right to work part-time – so, if you are a woman

wanting to work reduced hours because of your caring responsibilities, the legal routes open to you would be using indirect
discrimination arguments or the right to request flexible working.

The regulations are designed so that part-time workers are
not treated worse than full-timers when it comes to pay and
non-wage benefits. In order to bring a case you need to show
that you are being treated less favourably than a full-time worker
whom the law accepts as a valid comparator, and this is *because
of your part-time status*. Most workers are covered. It doesn't
matter whether you are temporary or full-time, an employee or
a worker. The right starts from your first day at work. As long as
there are workers doing a similar job, working longer hours
than you and getting better treatment, you can bring a case.

While only employees can claim unfair dismissal if they are
sacked for making a claim, everyone is protected against what the
law calls *detriment* such as being passed over for promotion –
because you have claimed your rights or helped a colleague to
claim under this law.

The regulations are broad in their scope and almost any term
or condition is covered, including:

- overtime pay (once the part-time employee has worked
  more than the normal full-time hours);
- contractual sick pay;
- access to any occupational pension scheme;
- training;
- holidays;
- maternity leave, pay and parental leave;
- access to career break schemes.

With whom can you compare yourself?

To be able to claim your rights under the regulations you have
to show that you have been treated less favourably than your
employer treated a full-time worker in similar circumstances.
You cannot compare yourself with just any worker. It has to be:

- a full-time worker, working for the same employer, in your own workplace;

- someone working under the same type of contract as you; and

- someone doing the same or similar work to yours.

If there is no full-time worker at your workplace who matches this description, you can choose someone from another of your employer's locations.

If you have been working full-time and shift to part-time work you can also compare your treatment with that which you previously enjoyed when you were full-time. For example, if you have taken maternity leave and it is agreed that you return to the same job but part-time, you should be able to keep your existing terms and conditions, pro rata to your working hours, unless your employer can justify the difference. You have this right to compare your situation to the one before you went on maternity leave provided you were not off for more than 12 months.

As long as there are full-time workers in your workplace doing generally the same work, you will be covered. If not, you will be able to compare yourself with full-time workers at another location, provided they have the same employer as you and are doing broadly similar work to yours.

But it is important to note that your full-time comparator must generally have the same type of contract as you. This means, for example, that if you are part-time and employed as an apprentice you cannot compare yourself to a full-time employee who is not an apprentice. However, you may still be able to compare yourself to a permanent full-timer even if you only have a fixed-term contract. You will need further advice on this.

Writing to your employer

Once you have found the eligible full-time worker (your comparator) who is being treated better than you, you should write to your employer and ask why you are being treated differently.

Before you do this, however, you should talk it through with an adviser, from your union if possible.

Once your employer has your letter, they have to reply within 21 days. If they do not, a tribunal can take this as evidence that your rights have been breached.

You will need to discuss their reply with your union or other adviser, to see if an employment tribunal is likely to accept your employer's arguments or side with you.

There are also similar rights for temporary workers not to be discriminated against in comparison with permanent workers. If you are a temporary worker suffering discrimination, contact your union representative or a legal or other specialist adviser.

Chapter Seven
Getting the sack

Dismissal

About the worst thing that can happen to you at work is losing your job. The legal term for getting the sack is dismissal. Your employer will tell you that you are no longer wanted and that from a certain date your employment will come to an end. At the end of this chapter you will find the dismissal maze. This is a table that will help you through the concepts in this chapter.

A dismissal can take place in a number of ways:

- Your employer can terminate your contract.
- Your job can be made redundant.
- Your employer can decide not to renew a fixed-term contract.
- In some circumstances, you can leave and claim that you were 'constructively dismissed'.

Notice

Your contract will normally say what notice your employer is required to give you if they intend to dismiss you. It will also normally say what notice you must give if you want to leave your job. The law does set out minimum standards for periods of notice, and the period of notice set out in your contract must not fall below the legal minimum notice period. Your employer must give you at least one week's notice after one month's employment, two weeks' notice after two years' employment, three weeks after three years, and so on up to 12 weeks after 12 years or more. Most employees are entitled to receive payment during this statutory notice period. If you are not given adequate notice of dismissal, you can sue the employer for 'wrongful dismissal' in a court or tribunal (see below and Chapter 8).

Once you have had your job for more than a month you must give at least one week's notice if you want to leave. This does not increase. However, your contract can set out a longer notice period for you to give to your employer.

Employers and employees can waive their right to notice or agree to a payment instead of receiving a period of notice (often called a 'payment in lieu of notice'). The law only allows such a payment if you agree to it or if it is allowed by terms in your contract. If your employer is keen for you to leave immediately, you may be able to use this to increase the payment you are given.

Either you or your employer can terminate the contract of employment without notice if the conduct of the other justifies it. You should only walk out if you believe that your employer is acting so badly that you feel you have no other option but to go, in which case you can make a claim for constructive dismissal (see below). Although you may be so desperate that you just want to quit on the spot, you should, if possible, take advice as to whether you have a good case. If you do walk out, your employer may deduct a week's wages or more from what is owing to you, as you have not given notice. You would have to win a constructive dismissal case to get this back.

Your employer can sack you without notice if you have been found guilty of gross misconduct, such as violence in the workplace, race discrimination or theft. Your employer is very likely to ask you to leave the premises immediately. Most contracts of employment will give examples of the types of behaviour considered to be gross misconduct and specify circumstances under which the employer may dismiss the employee without giving notice.

Written statement of reasons for dismissal

Once you have held your job for two years, your employer must give you a written statement of why you have been dismissed if you ask for it. The law says that this must be given in response to either a written or a verbal request, but it is always a good idea to put any communication with your employer about issues such as this in writing and keep a copy. The employer must provide this 'written statement for reasons of dismissal' – its legal name – within 14 days of your request.

If you get the sack while you are pregnant or on maternity leave, you should be given a written statement automatically. You should not have to ask for it and you should get one regardless of how long you have worked for your employer.

Constructive dismissal

A constructive dismissal may arise when your employer treats you so badly that you are convinced you have no alternative but to leave. This can occur, for example, if your employer makes major changes to your contract, or your job, without your consent and you find the changes unacceptable. Your employer's treatment of you must seriously undermine the contract between you. Your resignation must be tendered speedily and in response to the treatment. You must exercise great caution in resigning in this way, as it is extremely difficult to satisfy a court or tribunal that the circumstances made it impossible for you to continue. Even if you do convince the tribunal you will probably not get your old job back, but you could get compensation instead – though this may not be very much.

Wrongful dismissal

A wrongful dismissal occurs when you are dismissed in breach of your contract of employment, or against something provided for in your contract. It is not the same as an unfair dismissal, which is explained below.

Wrongful dismissals can include:

- a dismissal without proper notice;
- failure to pay your wages in full during the notice period; or
- any other breach of the provisions in your contract about notice.

As a claim for wrongful dismissal is a breach of contract claim, you can pursue your complaint in either the civil courts or an employment tribunal. Claims valued at £25,000 or under will usually be made in the employment tribunal, whereas those valued at over £25,000 may be brought in either a county court or the High Court (sheriff court or Court of Session in Scotland). A claim for wrongful dismissal to an employment tribunal must be made within three calendar months of the date of dismissal. For the civil courts there is a six-year period (five years in Scotland) following the dismissal within which you must make a claim.

The disadvantages of using the civil courts are that you will need legal representation and the costs of losing could be high if your former employer's costs are awarded against you. Employment tribunals are more informal, and costs awards are less likely to be made. You should take detailed advice about the best way to pursue a wrongful dismissal claim. It is hard to generalize, but it is likely that only high earners would be advised to take the riskier, though potentially more rewarding, route of a claim in the civil courts.

Unfair dismissal

If you are unfairly dismissed you can make a claim against your employer in the employment tribunal. If you have been dismissed and have also been discriminated against because of a 'protected characteristic' (see Chapter 6) or because of your trade union membership or activities, you can claim discrimination *and* unfair dismissal, which if successful may result in higher compensation.

Your dismissal may be unfair in one of three ways:

1 Your employer doesn't have a fair reason for dismissing you, eg your performance had improved but you were dismissed anyway.

2 Your employer didn't follow a fair procedure before dismissing you, eg you were dismissed without being given the opportunity to put forward your side of the story.

3 You were dismissed for an automatically unfair reason, eg because you took maternity leave.

Other than in some special cases set out on pages 184–185, you must have worked for your employer for more than two years to gain protection against unfair dismissal. You must also normally submit your claim within three calendar months of getting the sack.

Potentially fair reasons for dismissal

The law sets out the following potentially fair reasons for dismissal:

- (mis)conduct;
- capability or qualifications for the job;
- redundancy (your job is no longer needed);
- a legal requirement of the job that prevents the employment being continued;
- some other substantial reason that could justify the dismissal.

Conduct

Conduct covers your behaviour both on and, in some cases, off the job. For a dismissal on grounds of conduct to be considered fair, your employer would generally need to be able to show that they have conducted a proper investigation into your alleged misconduct and given you a chance to answer the case in a properly convened disciplinary hearing. The Employment Relations Act 1999 gave everyone involved in a disciplinary or grievance hearing the right to be accompanied by a fellow employee or a trade union representative, even if the employer does not recognize the union (see Chapter 5).

Some allowance is made for small businesses when considering the procedures used, as tribunals will expect higher standards from companies with full-time human resources or personnel officers. But small firms will still need to be able to show that they had established the facts of the case and given you a chance to respond, with representation if you wished, at a formal hearing before coming to the decision to dismiss you. You have the right to appeal against the dismissal and to be accompanied at an appeal hearing.

Your misconduct must also be sufficiently bad to justify dismissal. Misconduct outside the workplace can also be grounds for a fair dismissal. For example, it is likely that a tribunal would find dismissal of someone employed as a driver for a driving-related offence in his or her own car to be fair, but not the dismissal of someone who does not drive as part of his or her job. In other words, dismissal for an off-the-job offence must be shown to relate in some way to your job.

Clocking out for good

Euan Jones had worked for a food manufacturer for 22 years. He was sacked for clocking in electronically for a workmate who had slipped back to the cloakroom to collect a hair-cap that he had forgotten but that he had to wear for work. The employees' handbook listed clocking-in offences as among those regarded by the company as 'breaches of regulations [that] will result in instant dismissal'. There was also a notice above the reader that said 'It is a serious offence to use another employee's time card. Any irregularities must be reported immediately. Failure to do so means instant dismissal.' The last two words were written in large letters. Euan was seen using the workmate's card by witnesses and admitted to it.

Euan claimed unfair dismissal. His argument at the tribunal was that dismissal was too draconian a penalty after 22 years' service, and that a warning would have been more appropriate. But he lost. The tribunal decided that the dismissal was fair, as all staff had been given plenty of notice that a clocking-in offence would result in dismissal.

Tribunals have generally treated clocking-in offences with great severity. They have, on the whole, accepted employer arguments, reflected in many works rules, that clocking offences warrant instant dismissal. On the other hand, you may have a case if you can show that other workers were treated differently after committing the same offence, or that fiddling cards has been a common practice that everyone has previously ignored.

A tweet too far

The case *Game Retail v Laws* deals with some of the dangers of social media in the workplace. Mr Laws was responsible for approximately 100 of Game Retail's stores. He set up a personal Twitter account that he used to follow the stores for which he was responsible. A company employee reported that Laws had allegedly made several offensive, non-work-related comments. An investigation identified 28 offensive tweets. Laws was dismissed for gross misconduct.

The employment tribunal found the dismissal was unfair. It argued that Laws could not be identified as an employee of the company. Also, the employer's disciplinary policy was not sufficiently clear on the issue of whether the misuse of social media in private time could be treated as gross misconduct.

The employer appealed, and the employment appeal tribunal (EAT) found that the tribunal had not properly appreciated the public nature of Twitter. The comments could not be considered private, as they could be viewed by all the stores that followed Laws. This meant that the managers of those stores, and potentially customers, could have seen the offensive tweets. Added to this was the fact that Laws had failed to amend his privacy settings, so he knew that his comments could be seen by all his followers.

The EAT also found that there was no requirement to show that the tweets actually did cause offence. The employer only needed to show that the comments could have caused offence and that other staff or customers could have read them. Also, the EAT rejected the argument that it did not matter that the remarks did not relate to the company, or that Laws could not be identified as one of its employees.

More people succeed in employment tribunal cases by showing that their employer has failed to carry out fair procedures than by getting a tribunal to agree that their employer has over-reacted to misconduct. This is because the legal test they apply is whether a *reasonable employer* would dismiss a member of staff on these grounds. This is not the same as asking whether the misconduct is serious enough to justify dismissal, but whether other employers would do the same.

See Chapter 8 for more about employment tribunals and their procedures.

The pub lunch

Josh French worked on a passenger ferry. During one of his shifts he went to a pub to have lunch. He was joined by two workmates. The employers had a strict rule that employees should not enter licensed premises while working. A manager went to the pub and immediately suspended all three employees. There was no suggestion that Josh was drunk – he had merely gone to the most convenient place to obtain food – but his two colleagues acted in a way consistent with their being drunk. On the following day all three were summarily dismissed.

Management argued that, as all three had broken the same rule, all three must be punished equally. But Josh claimed unfair dismissal and won.

The tribunal took the view that there were enough differences between the conduct of Josh and that of his colleagues to make a reasonable employer distinguish between them. To treat all employees the same as a matter of course, without considering the particular circumstances of each individual, simply should not be done.

Many employers try to argue that there are some offences that warrant automatic penalties – no excuse being accepted. This case reinforces the argument that each individual case needs to be considered, and you should have the right to present your case in a disciplinary hearing.

Capability

A dismissal for capability is also potentially fair. For the first two years of your job you do not have any protection against unfair dismissal (except in the limited circumstances set out on pages 184–185), so your employer can sack you easily if they do not think you are up to the job during this time. Once you have worked for more than two years your employer will need to be able to show that, before dismissing you for capability, they had followed proper procedures to establish that you could not perform your job competently.

The most common situation giving rise to a dismissal for capability reasons is when your health deteriorates to the point that you cannot do your job any longer. However, your employer would need to show that they could not make changes in your working environment that would have allowed you to continue to work. The disability provisions of the Equality Act 2010 will be relevant in some cases (see Chapter 6).

Your employer will still have to follow a reasonable procedure, informing you that your job is at risk because of your capability, and arrange a meeting where you have the right to be accompanied, so that you can make representations.

Redundancy

You could be dismissed for redundancy if your employer needs to reduce the workforce for one of the following reasons:

- new technology, machinery or a new way of operating means that your job is no longer necessary;
- your job has been deleted, eg following a business reorganization;
- your employer has to reduce staff in order to cut costs;
- the business is moving or closing down.

Legally, it is the job that is made redundant, not the worker. This is a complex area covered in more detail on pages 187–192. If you are one of a group of workers doing more or less the same job and only some of you have been selected for redundancy, your employer must be able to show that the workers to be made redundant have been chosen fairly.

Dismissal on the grounds of redundancy will be deemed unfair if the employee is selected for redundancy, when others in the same circumstances are not, on grounds of:

- trade union membership or activities;
- taking certain types of action in relation to health and safety, for example refusing to do a job where the employee is convinced that there is a serious risk to his or her health and safety;
- any reason in connection with maternity;
- asserting a statutory right, for example asking to be paid the minimum wage;
- refusing to do shop or betting work on Sundays (see Chapter 5);
- acting as an employees' representative in relation to consultation on redundancies or a business transfer;
- performing any duties relating to an employee's role as an occupational pension fund trustee.

Dismissal on the grounds of redundancy may also be unfair if your employer has not given you adequate warning of it or if they have failed to consider offering you another job.

Legal requirement

A typical example of this would be getting the sack from a job as a driver because you have lost your licence. However, your employer must also show that there is no alternative employment with the company.

Some other substantial reason

Unfortunately the law does not define what is meant by 'some other substantial reason' (SOSR), but the reason must be serious and justify your dismissal. Tribunals have devised various tests to help them decide whether or not a dismissal was for a 'substantial' reason. Examples of dismissals found to have been for SOSR include: where an employee is excluded from the workplace by the employer's client; and where a temporary worker employed to cover someone on maternity leave is dismissed upon the return of the employee. Ultimately the tribunal has to decide, based on all the relevant facts of the case, whether the reason justified the dismissal. It will consider whether or not any grievance or disciplinary procedures were properly used. In these circumstances, it is particularly important for employees to ensure that they ask for written reasons for dismissal, as described above.

Shifting a shift?

Two security staff, Amy Adams and John Pollard, were asked to change shift patterns, as their employer thought this would lead to more efficient use of staff time. After consultation both refused and were sacked. Amy had been with the firm less than a year so could not make a claim, but John was a long-serving employee, and his wife was currently ill, which is why he didn't want to change. He claimed unfair dismissal, but lost.

The tribunal agreed that their refusal to change their shift patterns harmed the business interests of their employer. John's dismissal was therefore a potentially fair dismissal under the category 'some other substantial reason'.

This shows that in some circumstances you cannot rely on your contract of employment. The tribunal will usually concentrate on whether the employee was 'reasonable' in resisting change, and whether the employer was 'reasonable' in insisting on the change. If the employer can show an overriding business need for the change, the tribunal will tend to decide in the employer's favour.

Qualifying conditions

If you think you have been unfairly dismissed, you may complain to an employment tribunal. In most circumstances, you must be an 'employee' (see the Introduction) and have worked continuously for two years for the same employer. Members of the police force and armed forces cannot claim unfair dismissal. The qualifying period is not always necessary. It is reduced to one month where you are dismissed on medical grounds because of some health and safety requirements. There is no length of service requirement at all to make a complaint of unfair dismissal if you are sacked because:

- You are pregnant, or for any reason connected with maternity.

- You are a trade union member or because of trade union activity (or because you have refused to join a union).

- You have taken some action to enforce your workplace rights – 'seeking to assert a statutory right' in legal jargon. A common cause is asking to receive a written statement of employment particulars after two months of employment.

- You have refused to do something on health and safety grounds (see pages 122–128 for details on what you can and cannot refuse to do).

- You have 'blown the whistle' on malpractice in the workplace (see pages 31–32).

- You have refused or are proposing to refuse to do shop work or work connected with betting on a Sunday (see pages 24–25).

- You are acting as a representative of employees for consultation on redundancy or a business transfer, or have put yourself forward as a candidate to do this. This might happen in a workplace where there is no recognized trade union, as in some circumstances an employer must organize elections for workforce representatives so that they can consult with their staff.

- You are an employee pension fund trustee or proposing to become one and have been sacked because of your role.

- You have represented a fellow worker at a grievance or disciplinary hearing, or you have asked to bring a fellow worker or a trade union representative with you to such a hearing.

- You have campaigned for or against statutory trade union recognition.

- You have taken part in lawful industrial action and have been dismissed for doing so within the first 12 weeks of that action.

You must complete the Acas early conciliation process before you can make a complaint of unfair dismissal to a tribunal. Unfair dismissal claims must be lodged within three calendar months of the 'effective date of termination' of your employment (usually the date of leaving the job) or within one month of the date shown on the early conciliation certificate sent to you by Acas. Tribunals do have the power to consider claims made late if they consider that it was not 'reasonably practicable' for you to get the claim in on time, but in practice they are very reluctant to do this. It is always best to tell Acas soon after your dismissal that you want to make a claim, which costs £250 to lodge, as it might be possible to reach an agreement with your employer to settle without having to go to tribunal.

Tribunal procedures are explained in more detail in Chapter 8, which also sets out a number of alternative ways of settling a case, either before or after you have made a claim, that do not involve the stress of a full hearing, and these are certainly worth considering.

If you do proceed to a hearing for unfair dismissal, a tribunal will first establish that you were an employee and that you have been dismissed. It will then consider whether the reason given by your employer for dismissing you is one of the potentially fair reasons for dismissal, before moving on to consider whether your employer acted reasonably in all the circumstances, ie followed a fair procedure, in dismissing you for that reason. Should the tribunal decide that your dismissal was unfair, it will consider ordering one of three possible remedies – reinstatement, re-engagement or compensation. If an order for reinstatement or re-engagement is made you are entitled to the lost earnings in the period between the dismissal and the reinstatement (see Chapter 8 for more details). The difference between reinstatement and re-engagement is that reinstatement gives you your old job back, while re-engagement gives you a different, but comparable, job.

As a result of age discrimination laws, you can now claim unfair dismissal whatever age you are. If you have been dismissed because you have reached the 'normal retiring age' for your workplace, your employer will have to show the dismissal was objectively justifiable.

There is no specified lower age limit for claiming, although it is illegal to work when you are under 13. Those defined by their employers as 'apprentices' cannot be dismissed unless their contract specifically says that they can be.

Geographical limits

If you are employed outside the UK but the employment relationship is closely connected with Great Britain – for example, if the employer conducts their business in Great Britain, you are regularly working overseas but your contract specifies the UK as your base, or if you are working in a British 'enclave' such as a military base – you may still be able to claim unfair dismissal.

There are special regulations relating to those employed offshore, that is, on ships or oil rigs. UK workers posted in EU countries are entitled to all the employment protection that applies to nationals of the particular country in which they are working. This area of the law is complex. If you are working abroad or working in the UK for a foreign-owned company you should take further advice from your union or one of the sources listed in Chapter 9 about making a claim for unfair dismissal.

Redundancy

Redundancy is sometimes used as a polite word for getting the sack, but it has a precise legal meaning and you have special rights if you are made redundant. In particular, many have a right to redundancy pay. A redundancy is a dismissal caused by the employer's need to reduce their workforce. It may come about because a workplace is closing down, the way things are done has been restructured or reorganized, or fewer employees of a particular kind are (or are expected to be) needed.

Normally, your job will be deleted, so it's unlikely to be a redundancy if your employer immediately takes on someone else to do your job. This does not mean that your employer cannot take on workers of a different type, or at some other location (unless the redundant employees could be required under their contracts to move to the new location). It could still be redundancy if someone else already working for your employer moves into your old job (sometimes called 'bumping') as long as there is an overall loss of jobs. If you have worked for your employer for at least two years continuously, you may be entitled to a redundancy payment. See below for further information on how redundancy pay is calculated.

Where your original job has been deleted, you may be able to avoid dismissal if your employer or an associated employer offers you another job. This is known as 'redeployment'; however, to avoid dismissal you must be offered the new job before your old contract expires. If you are offered redeployment but you're not sure whether the job is suitable, you are entitled to work in the new job on a trial basis for four weeks. If, during the trial period, it is apparent that the job is unsuitable, you can turn it down or agree with your employer (in writing) to extend the trial period. If you reject the new job before the end of the trial period, because it is an unsuitable alternative to your old job or for good personal reasons, your entitlement to a redundancy payment (if any) will not be affected and your employment will terminate at the end of the notice period.

However, if your employer argues that the job is suitable you may need to make a claim to a tribunal and show the tribunal why the job was not suitable. If the tribunal finds you unreasonably refused a suitable offer of alternative employment you lose your right to a redundancy payment.

You should think carefully before turning down an alternative job, even if you believe it is unsuitable. It might be worth trying to agree with your employer to extend the trial period, eg to allow more time for retraining. If at the end of the trial period you are still in the job, you will be deemed to have accepted it. This means that you lose any rights to claim a redundancy payment.

Contract not renewed

Liz Acott was a lecturer at a college of further education. Her appointment was for one academic year, and was not renewed. This was not a surprise. There had always been doubt that there would be enough money in her department's budget to renew her contract at the end of the period of appointment. But when her appointment was not renewed Liz claimed unfair dismissal.

The tribunal said that Liz's job was redundant, and redundancy can be a fair reason for dismissal. But they also held that the employer had a duty, as in any other redundancy situation, to try to assist Liz by considering her for other jobs they might have available. Since there was no evidence that the college had done this, she won her case.

What can you get?

The law provides a legal minimum for redundancy pay. Some employers will offer better terms, and some will include these in your contract of employment. The legal minimum depends on the length of your continuous service with your employer, how old you are and how much you are paid:

- For each complete year of employment after your 41st birthday you should get one and a half weeks' pay.

- For each complete year of employment after your 22nd birthday but before you turn 41 you should get one week's pay.

- For each complete year of employment while you were either 18, 19, 20 or 21 you should get half a week's pay.

Unless your employer or contract of employment is more generous, you cannot claim more than 20 years' worth of redundancy payments.

If you are made redundant you are entitled to a minimum period of notice. This is one week for every whole year you have worked for your employer up to a maximum of 12 weeks. If your employer makes, or lets, you leave before this minimum period of notice you should still be 'paid in lieu' for the remaining notice period.

Working out how many years of service you have in order to calculate your redundancy payment is far from simple. The period starts with your first day with your current employer, and ends at what is called the 'relevant date'. This is the day on which your redundancy notice expires, even if your employer has let, or made, you stop work in the meantime.

It is calculated in calendar years, but with no fractions of a year. If you have worked for 10 years and 11 months, then it is counted as 10 whole years. You must have worked continuously in the employment. While days on strike do not count towards the total, they do not break the continuity of the employment. Periods of maternity or parental leave do count and do not break the continuity of employment. Other absences may sometimes count towards a period of continuous employment, even where the employment contract was broken, for example by a temporary stoppage of work or if you move from one contract to another with the same employer or between two different employers within the same sector, such as within local government or the NHS.

Calculating a week's pay

The week's wage is taken to be what your contract of employment said you should have been paid in the week your employer gave you notice, for that week's work. If for some reason your employer did not give you formal notice, it is the week in which they should have given you notice.

If you don't have normal working hours, your pay will vary from week to week. For example, you may be paid on a piece-work basis. So, if you are being made redundant, you should use the last 12 full weeks you worked leading up to the day you were given notice of your redundancy. Overtime and other bonuses can count if you are guaranteed them in your contract of employment. If you received no pay for one week during the 12-week period then you need to count back a week.

There is an upper limit of how much your weekly pay can be taken to be for the purposes of working out your redundancy pay. At the time of writing the limit was £475. It is uprated each year, normally in line with the Retail Price Index.

Your employer may offset part of your company pension payment against your redundancy payment if you are dismissed not more than 90 weeks before the first pension payment is due.

Currently you do not have to pay tax on a statutory redundancy payment, but that may change in the future. Nor does a payment affect your right to claim unemployment benefit. You will not be entitled to statutory redundancy pay if any of the following apply:

- You are an apprentice whose service ends at the end of your apprenticeship contract.

- You are on a fixed-term contract of more than two years' duration that includes, with your written agreement, a clause waiving your right to a redundancy payment, provided your employment ended at the appointed time.

- You are a domestic servant working in a private household and you are a member of the employer's immediate family.

- You are a share fisherman paid solely by a share of the catch.

- You are a crown servant or employee in a public office or in the NHS covered by other redundancy arrangements.

- You are an employee of the government of an overseas territory.

If your employer is in financial difficulty, the payment is made by the Insolvency Service (out of the National Insurance Fund), but only the statutory minimum can be paid, and there are limits on the number of weeks for which payment can be claimed. If you have lost out because of a difference between the statutory minimum redundancy pay and what your contract offered, you can make a claim against the remaining assets of the business, but a bankrupt company may not have sufficient assets to pay.

Liability for making the payment rests with your employer, but if administrators or receivers have been appointed to wind up the business you can ask them to give you form RP1, which you should complete and forward to the Insolvency Service as soon as possible after you've been dismissed. The Insolvency Service can make payments for redundancy pay, unpaid wages and holiday pay (maximum amounts apply).

There is no need for you to make an employment tribunal claim unless your employer fails to pay you statutory redundancy pay or disputes the entitlement. Where this happens, you should make a written request to your employer or refer the matter to an employment tribunal, or both, within six calendar months of the date your employment ended. If you do not claim within six months you may lose the right to a payment, but the tribunal has discretion to extend this period by a further six months.

Consultation on redundancy

If your employer proposes to make 20 or more people redundant they must, by law, consult the workforce. If your employer recognizes a trade union they must consult with union representatives. If no union is recognized your employer must consult with an established representative body such as a staff forum or association, if there is one, and if not they must consult with employee representatives, elected by the entire workforce.

An employer must consult about ways of avoiding redundancies, reducing the numbers affected and lessening their effect. Agreement does not have to be reached as a result of the consultation, but the employer must consult 'in good faith', that is, with a view to reaching agreement. Certain information must be disclosed to the representative body, including:

- the reasons for the redundancies;

- the numbers and descriptions of those affected;

- how any redundancy payments better than the legal minimum will be worked out.

Consultation cannot just take place one afternoon when the managing director has a spare half-hour. There are minimum periods during which representatives must be consulted. Where it is proposed that 20 to 99 employees will be dismissed at one establishment over a period of 90 days or less, consultation must last at least 30 days, and if it is proposed that 100 or more employees will be dismissed as above, consultation must last at least 45 days. It doesn't matter that fewer than 20 (or 100) are actually dismissed, as some may have been redeployed or taken voluntary redundancy; if the employer's proposal places more than 20 (or 100) at risk of redundancy, consultation must take place.

Individual notices of redundancy should not be issued until after consultation has ended – in line with these requirements. Any complaint that redundancy notices have been issued before consultation has ended can be made to an employment tribunal. If the tribunal finds that a complaint is justified it can make a protective award, which will require the employer to pay the employees their normal pay for the period covered by the protective award – usually 90 days. This is to allow for the consultation to take place before the redundancies are made.

Follow a path through the dismissal maze to find out your basic rights:

Are you an employee?

Not all workers are employees. As well as the obviously self-employed, other workers can find that they are not employees in the strict legal sense – see pages 10–12.

Yes   No

➤   ➤ There's probably nothing you can do, but it may be worth seeking further advice based on your own circumstances.

Have you lost your job because:

you are pregnant;

of your sex, race, disability, age, religious belief or sexual orientation;

you refused to undertake dangerous or unsafe activities that posed a threat of physical injury;

you tried to join a union;

you 'blew the whistle' on wrongdoing at work;

you asserted your right to be paid the minimum wage or took action against your employer for a breach of employment law?

No   Yes

➤   ➤ You have probably been unfairly dismissed.

You can take a case to an employment tribunal. It does not matter how long you have worked for your current employer – all dismissals on these grounds are automatically unfair (though employers will normally say that dismissal was for another reason).

Have you worked for your employer for more than two years?

Yes

No

▶ There may be nothing you can do. Unless your dismissal came about through one of the special cases above, your employer can dismiss you without saying why. However, you should look at your contract of employment. If this contains procedures such as notice periods or the promise of a formal hearing that were not followed then you may very well have a case. Seek advice.

Does your employer say you are being made redundant?

No

Yes

▶ Think carefully about the reasons given. A job will not have ended in a 'bumping' situation (see above) and, in some circumstances, following a business reorganization, for example where duties and responsibilities are subsumed by other staff across the business or where the employer requires the same work to be carried out differently.

Employers may select people for redundancy, but they cannot discriminate on grounds of sex, race, disability, age, religious belief or sexual orientation.

If there are any procedures for redundancy in your contract of employment then these must be followed.

If there are more than 20 redundancies then your employer must consult with the workforce. If there is a recognized union this must be with union representatives. If there is no union then special representatives must be elected. The consultation allows representatives to argue that the company should think again, to change the criteria by which people are selected for redundancy (say by increasing redundancy pay or early retirement pensions and asking for volunteers) and/or to argue for more help such as training or job search for those who are to go.

Has your employer followed these procedures properly?

You may have a case. Take advice.

No   Yes

►   ▲

► You are entitled to redundancy pay if you have worked for your employer for more than two years. The amount depends on your age, length of service and pay. Many employers will be more generous than these legal minimums: aged 18–21 – half a week's pay for each year of service; aged 22–40 – one week's pay for each year of service; aged 41 or over – one and a half weeks' pay for each year of service.

But weekly pay of more than £475 is not counted, and no more than 20 years' service can be taken into account.

Have you lost your job because:

you cannot do it properly;

of serious misconduct by you;

of some legal requirement?

No   Yes

►   ▲

If your employer cannot prove that you have been dismissed for one of these reasons then you have been unfairly dismissed.

► As long as your employer has followed proper procedures then you can be fairly dismissed for any of these reasons.

However, if you have any doubts you should take advice. You may have a successful tribunal case if an employer has not got a fair system for judging conduct or capability. Any employee facing a disciplinary hearing can take a workmate or union official in with him or her. If this is denied then you may have a case.

A tribunal may also disagree with an employer's judgement that your misconduct was serious enough to be punished by dismissal or that you could not do your job properly.

Chapter Eight
Enforcing your rights

Employers may deny you your legal rights for a number of reasons. They may simply not understand the law or fully appreciate their responsibilities as employers. While this is no excuse, there are often changes in employment law that some employers may not have kept up to date with, or they may not fully understand some of the finer points of complex provisions such as shared parental leave. Once someone points out their legal obligations, however, they are unlikely to continue to deny you your rights.

Other employers know that they are breaking the law but hope they can get away with it. If challenged, they too are likely to back down. Sometimes anonymous letters have allowed workforces to challenge this type of employer without having to identify a 'ringleader'.

In other cases your employer may genuinely believe that they are acting correctly and within the law, but you, and your advisers, may disagree. Some of these cases arise because there is room for more than one point of view, such as whether your misconduct was serious enough to get you the sack. These cases may end up in a tribunal, or be settled through one of the alternatives to a tribunal hearing described below. In other cases the law may not be clear, and a test case will be necessary to settle not just your case but that of many other people in your position.

One example of this process is in relation to the holiday pay litigation in which the unions played a part in establishing that holiday pay should be calculated taking account of overall earnings and not just basic pay. For many workers in the UK pay is composed of several different elements such as overtime, unsociable hours payments and shift premiums that historically employers have ignored when determining holiday pay. This left many workers substantially worse off when taking paid leave. It is now clear that holiday pay must take into account all elements of pay that are linked to the performance of the tasks that the employee is required to do, including certain types of overtime.

But it is a different matter when you are taking on a company that deliberately exploits and bullies its staff. If it has sacked you unfairly, you have nothing to lose in taking action against it. But if you want to enforce your rights while still an employee you need to understand that, even when the law is on your side, a vindictive employer can still do a great deal to make your life miserable, particularly if you are acting on your own.

You do need to think through your options very carefully if you are in this position, and as we stress in so many parts of this book you should take further advice. While the law is likely to be on your side (as soon as you take action to enforce your rights, you gain special protection against unfair dismissal, even if you have only just started working for your employer), there may be better ways to proceed, such as signing up fellow employees into a trade union and asking them to act on your behalf collectively so that the employer cannot identify and victimize anyone. Some breaches of employment law can be investigated by external agencies such as the Health and Safety Executive (HSE) or HMRC's national minimum wage enforcement team, and you may want to call them in. More information on what enforcement agencies can do to protect your employment rights can be found at **www.gov.uk**.

Another route to settling an employment law issue is to go to mediation, which can be an early way of resolving a dispute before it escalates to a job loss or a potential tribunal claim. For more on mediation, and for the difference between that and conciliation or arbitration, go to **www.acas.org.uk/mediation**.

If you do decide, after taking advice, that you need to take legal action, there are a number of different courts and tribunals that can hear claims relating to employment rights. Each has an appeal route if you or your employer wishes to appeal against a decision. In the case of work-related welfare benefits, such as Statutory Sick Pay, claims are dealt with by a separate system of tribunals (see Chapter 2).

Employment tribunals and the courts

Bodies known as employment tribunals deal with most work-related legal action. Employment tribunals operate in England, Wales and Scotland. In Northern Ireland the system is similar, but the tribunals are called industrial tribunals. Separate fair employment tribunals hear claims relating to discrimination, including on the basis of political opinion, which is illegal in Northern Ireland.

These tribunals are specialist employment 'courts'. A tribunal will often be made up of three people. The employment judge is legally qualified, and there may be two lay members, one of whom has been chosen as an employee representative and the other as an employer representative. As a panel, all members must exercise impartiality, but the lay members will be expected to bring their employment experience to bear when judging the facts of the case. Increasingly, in more straightforward cases, the employment judge will sit alone, particularly when there are any preliminary legal arguments. Employment tribunals are serviced by regional offices of Her Majesty's Court Service (HMCS), and hearings take place at regional venues.

Tribunals were originally intended to provide a relatively cheap, speedy and informal means of settling employment rights disputes between employees and employers. While they are still less formal than civil courts, the introduction of fees has made it harder for many workers to bring tribunal claims. Those who have may find tribunals have become more legalistic and formal as the law has become more complex.

However, most claims at tribunals are about unfair dismissal. Argument is therefore normally about the facts of the matter, rather than legal points, and you do not necessarily need legal representation – a union officer or advice worker, particularly if he or she has been advising you throughout the dispute, may know the case better.

Civil courts

Not all employment-related cases go to a tribunal, and sometimes you can choose from a number of options. As we saw in Chapter 7, if you have been wrongfully dismissed – rather than unfairly dismissed – you can either take a case to a tribunal or pursue it through the civil courts. While tribunals can hear claims of breach of contract where the employment has ended or where financial loss has occurred that amounts to an unlawful deduction from wages, civil courts can hear claims for breach of contract that do not involve dismissal, for example if you suffer a financial loss because your employer changes your contract without your agreement.

These courts can also hear claims for personal injury if you are injured in the workplace or suffer ill health as a result of your working environment and want to sue your employer for damages. For personal injury claims, you will need specialized legal help, so we do not go into any detail here. Your union will probably have an arrangement with a firm of specialist lawyers and will pick up any legal costs. If you win, costs are likely to be awarded against the employer. If you are not in a union, a local advice agency will be able to recommend solicitors who specialize in personal injury cases. Many solicitors will take such cases on a 'no win, no fee' basis if they think you have a good case. We would advise you to beware 'claims farms' companies that advertise in newspapers and on television. Some make inflated claims about what they can achieve.

A few employment-related matters might go to the criminal courts. For example, the HSE can prosecute employers who breach health and safety law, and HMRC's national minimum wage enforcement team can prosecute employers for failure to pay the NMW or for failing to keep or falsifying their records. And if you do something illegal at work, such as stealing, or assaulting a colleague, you may be liable to criminal prosecution.

Where do I make my claim?

It is sometimes difficult to know *where* to pursue a claim. The rule of thumb is to check first to see whether the problem is covered by the list of issues dealt with by employment tribunals (see below). Claims are usually lodged in the tribunal located closest to your place of work, even if that is some distance from where you live. Claims must be made on an ET1 form, which can be downloaded from the Justice website: **www.justice.gov.uk**.

You can make a claim at an employment tribunal under several 'heads'. For example, if your boss reduces your wages without your consent and then sacks you without notice when you complain then you can claim wrongful dismissal and unauthorized deduction from wages.

Some disputes are not so easy to define. Common examples are disputes involving stress and bullying at work (see Chapter 5). You cannot pursue a claim of 'bullying' to an employment tribunal, but sometimes these issues are directly related to another issue that *can* be taken to a tribunal. Stress may be due to long hours, and working time issues can be taken to a tribunal. Bullying may include a discrimination aspect if it is related to one of the protected characteristics, and this too can be taken to a tribunal.

Often it will not be so simple. You can, however, sometimes rely on the 'implied' duty in your contract of employment for your employer to provide a healthy and safe working environment (see Chapter 5). For example, if you are constantly being picked on by an aggressive line manager for no obvious reason, and your complaints to more senior management have been ignored, you can try to sue in either a county court or the High Court, depending on the level of compensation you wish to claim.

Such cases are often complex, and you are advised to seek help. A trade union will have expertise in assessing your problem and looking for redress in the right place. If you are not a union member, you could take independent legal advice, perhaps from a law centre. If you cannot obtain free advice, you may have to pay a lawyer or other adviser for assistance. However, legal advice and representation may be available free of charge through your union, so if you are not already a member it makes sense to join.

You cannot pursue the same claim in two courts at the same time even if both have the power to decide your claim. The term 'court' here includes employment tribunals. Neither can you bring a claim again in another court after you have lost it in the first one.

Claims can be heard against employers who are based outside the UK as long as you are ordinarily resident in the UK. If you are a citizen of another EU country posted in the UK, you can claim protection under UK law and submit a claim to an employment tribunal or court. Similarly, if you are a UK national working in an EU country you are covered by its employment protection and can make a claim in its courts.

It may be that you do not want to go to court or to an employment tribunal, in which case you could try to negotiate a settlement of the matter with your employer. This is covered in more detail later on in this chapter.

Cases dealt with by employment tribunals

These are the main areas of employment law dealt with by tribunals:

- equal pay;
- sex, pregnancy and maternity discrimination;
- discrimination because of transgender status;
- discrimination on the basis of marriage or civil partnership status;
- race discrimination;
- disability discrimination;
- business transfers and 'service provision changes';
- discrimination on the basis of age, religious belief or sexual orientation;
- discrimination on the basis of trade union membership/non-membership or activities;
- time off rights for pension fund trustees or trade union and safety representatives;
- wages issues, including the national minimum wage and unlawful deductions;
- wrongful dismissal (breach of contract);
- unfair dismissal;
- redundancy;
- 'whistle-blowing';
- working time and part-time working;
- the right to be accompanied, or to accompany a colleague, at a disciplinary or grievance hearing in the workplace;
- the right to campaign for or against trade union recognition;
- dismissal for taking lawful industrial action;

- maternity leave, paternity leave, adoption leave, shared parental leave, parental leave and leave for family emergencies;
- dismissal for asserting a statutory right;
- written statement of employment particulars;
- written reasons for dismissal;
- failure to consider reasonably an employee's application to work flexibly.

Making a claim

Where your claim is about anything other than an actual dismissal, in most cases it is advisable to put your complaint in writing (grievance) to your employer before bringing a claim in the employment tribunal. This is to encourage you and your employer to try to resolve things in the workplace without the need to go to a tribunal. If you are a union member you can seek help from your union representative with putting in your grievance.

It is not difficult to make a claim to an employment tribunal, but before doing so you must notify Acas of your complaint. Acas will offer you and your employer help with settling the dispute (known as early conciliation). You won't be allowed to lodge a claim unless you have contacted Acas, but neither you nor your employer has to take part in conciliation.

Once you have notified Acas, the time for lodging a claim in the tribunal will be extended, in some cases by up to six weeks, so if you're unable to reach agreement you still have time to lodge a claim.

You can notify Acas by telephone (0300 123 1100) or by completing an online notification form (**www.acas.org.uk/ earlyconciliation**). If no agreement to settle the dispute can be reached, Acas will send you a certificate. Your claim must reach the tribunal within one month of the date shown on the certificate.

The next step is to fill out a form called an ET1. These are readily and freely available from the Justice website **www.justice.gov.uk**, where you can download, complete and send the form by e-mail. ET1 forms are also available from a Jobcentre, Acas, your union, a local advice agency or the regional or national employment tribunal offices (see Chapter 9). Although these forms are not difficult to fill in, it is very important to ensure that nothing that will help your case is left out and nothing that will damage your case is included.

On 29 July 2013, the government changed significantly the way in which employment tribunals operate by introducing fees.

You have to pay two fees – one at the start of a claim (an issue fee) and one before the case is heard by the tribunal (a hearing fee). The amount depends on the type of claim. The issue fee for straightforward claims like redundancy payment, breach of contract or unlawful deductions from wages is £160 (these are called type A claims), whereas to start a claim for unfair dismissal, discrimination and whistle-blowing, which are normally more complex claims (type B claims), the fee is £250. Likewise, the hearing fee for a type A claim is £230, and for a type B claim it is £950. Different levels of fee apply if your claim is one of a number of similar claims being brought by a group of workers against the same employer. Separate fees also apply for appeals to the employment appeals tribunal.

It is perhaps unsurprising that far fewer claims have been lodged in the employment tribunal since fees were introduced. The government has faced strong criticism from unions, charities and lawyers for preventing workers from seeking justice.

If you have a good claim but can't afford the fees, you might qualify for full or partial exemption from the fees, depending on your financial circumstances. You can find out more about exemption from fees (called remission) from the Justice website: **www.gov.uk/employment-tribunals/when-you-can-claim**.

Seek help from your trade union or from a Citizens Advice Bureau (CAB). While a CAB will give free assistance with filling out the form and general advice on your claim, it cannot represent you at the tribunal. Your union will normally provide representation if it considers that your claim is likely to succeed, though it may not take forward cases that it considers weak. This is not an assessment of whether or not you have been treated badly by your employer, but an opinion on whether you will succeed at the tribunal. These are two quite different issues. Once you have submitted the ET1 you will become known as the 'claimant'.

It is crucial that you submit the claim within the legal time limits. For most cases, claims must be made within three calendar months of the 'effective date of termination' (usually the day on which you finish work) or the problem happening, but there are some variations depending on what the complaint is. See the timetable on pages 41–49 for all the time limits. It is very hard to persuade a tribunal to accept a claim that is 'out of time', even if only by a day. It is worth using recorded delivery so that you can prove when you posted the claim, in case it arrives late because of postal difficulties beyond your control. You can also lodge the claim by e-mail or fax, but if you do not receive an acknowledgement in return you may need to telephone the tribunal to check that the claim has been received.

There is no legal aid available for representation at employment tribunals, although basic preliminary advice, for example on whether discrimination has occurred, can sometimes be obtained under the Legal Help scheme. This provides a short session with a solicitor to talk through any legal issue on a preliminary basis. Costs are not automatically awarded in the tribunal but may be awarded if the tribunal considers that your claim was 'misconceived', that is, had no reasonable prospects of succeeding but was pursued anyway. If you are in doubt as to the strength of your claim you may wish to take advice, as tribunals now have the power to order that you pay the employer's legal costs up to £20,000. The tribunal may decide to award costs based on the amount of time spent by you or your employer on preparing your cases. In addition, if you pay some-body to represent you at the tribunal and he or she wastes time and is incompetent, he or she may be liable to costs. This will not apply if he or she is representing you for nothing, for example if you are represented by a trade union official or advice agency worker.

It is possible to represent yourself at a tribunal. The panel hearing the case will try to help you. Although some people do successfully represent themselves, particularly in simpler cases, it is always best to try to have your own representative who is familiar with the way tribunals work. This is particularly important if your employer is going to be legally represented, and many are. You do not necessarily need to be represented by a lawyer. Union full-time officers are very experienced in taking cases to tribunals, although some unions now operate a policy of sending out all employment work to their panel solicitors. If you are not in a union, you can consider employing your own solicitor, although as costs are not usually awarded at tribunals you will not normally be able to claim legal costs back from the other side if you win. Some advice agencies may be able to provide someone to represent you.

On the ET1 you will be asked to indicate the type of claim(s) you are asking the tribunal to decide. This will be one or more from the list above, for example unfair dismissal and sex dis-crimination. You do not need to name the correct law, although if you can it does have the advantage of making the basis of your complaint absolutely clear to the tribunal.

You will also need to give details of the complaint and the remedy you are seeking. With any dismissal case you are advised to ask for reinstatement or re-engagement. You are highly unlikely to get it – on average less than 1 per cent of claims result in reinstatement or re-engagement – but it seems to have the effect of increasing the compensation, which you will probably get instead. It is also worth stating that you would like your claim to be heard by the full panel, as tribunals are increasingly trying to hear claims, at least at the preliminary stages, with the employment judge sitting on his or her own. The advantage of the full panel is that there will be one member who has direct experience of your 'side' of the argument, and you may get a more balanced decision at least on the facts.

You must be clear about whom the claim is against. After receiving the ET1, the tribunal can ask you to give a written answer to a question if it thinks that this would provide helpful clarification. It is important that you do this if you are asked, as it may help your case.

The ET1 has to be sent to the employment tribunal's office nearest to the employer's business (the address is given on the form, and a helpful guidance booklet will be enclosed with the form). Your form and an ET2, which is a summons, are sent to the employer, who is known as the 'respondent'. Bear in mind that the employer will see everything that you have written on your form, as will the tribunal panel, so be clear, be accurate and be polite! The employer then has to return an ET3 form, known as a 'response form', in which they will set out their defence.

Most employment rights are subject to eligibility requirements. The tribunal will first check that you are eligible to bring the case you have submitted. If there is any doubt, there will be a preliminary hearing, usually involving just the employment judge.

For example, to claim unfair dismissal, you must be an 'employee' in legal terms and normally have worked continuously for your employer for two years, and you must send the form in within three calendar months of the 'effective date of termination' (normally your last day at work). The three-month time limit might be extended if you have been trying to resolve the dispute with your employer with help from Acas (see page 185 on early conciliation). If you do not meet any of these conditions, the tribunal will reject your claim. Each chapter of this book explains the eligibility requirements in each case, and Table 1.1 on pages 41–49 gives a timetable showing the time limits for each type of claim. If the tribunal decides that your case has no reasonable chance of success, it can hold a preliminary hearing, at which it may require you to pay a deposit of up to £500, which you will lose if you lose the case.

How tribunals work

There is a complex set of rules governing tribunal procedures, and tribunals currently have considerable discretion in how to handle cases. You should provide as much supporting written evidence to your employer (or their representative) in advance of your hearing as possible. The tribunal calls this 'disclosure'. The tribunal can order both you and the employer to provide more evidence if it wants. It normally expects to see items such as written warnings, statements from witnesses, copies of the company disciplinary procedure and pay statements. Either you or the employer may ask the tribunal to order disclosure of documents before the hearing if you feel that they are necessary to make a fair decision. The tribunal can also make witness orders, requiring witnesses for you or the employer to attend.

The tribunal will normally try to meet within six months from when you first submitted your ET1. It could take longer if your case involves more than one claim or is complex. It will tell you and your employer when the hearing is due. You or the employer can apply for a postponement if there is a genuine difficulty with the required time. Most tribunal hearings are held in large rooms rather than formal courtrooms. The three members of the panel will sit at the front, with the parties to the case and their representatives sitting opposite on the front row of chairs, with others behind. Tribunal hearings are open to the public unless a specific request is made to the tribunal for a closed hearing and the tribunal agrees to this. This is normally only done in cases of great sensitivity, for example involving sexual harassment, or where there are implications for national security.

An important consideration for the way the case proceeds is where the burden of proof lies. In some cases the onus is on you to show that your employer acted unlawfully. In others it is up to the employer to show they acted lawfully. For example, if you have been dismissed while you are pregnant, it is entirely up to the employer to show that they had good reason, other than reasons related to pregnancy, to sack you. In other words, the tribunal will assume that you were dismissed because of your pregnancy unless your employer can prove that they sacked you for another, potentially fair reason, eg poor performance. In other cases (such as constructive dismissal) the burden of proof is with you, and you therefore have to prove that your employer was in the wrong.

Your witness evidence will be taken 'as read', which means that you will not be asked to read out your statement before the other side asks questions in cross-examination. The tribunal will then examine the documentation and finally call for closing statements from both parties. The tribunal can adjourn the hearing if time runs out or if either party wants to consider a settlement out of court at any time during the hearing. It can also stop proceedings if the respondent decides to concede the case or if the tribunal decides that one party or the other is the clear winner and nothing would be gained by continuing the hearing. The panel will then decide whether you have won the case and if so what compensation or other award you should receive. Each member of the three-person tribunal has an equal say, so it is possible for the lay members to outvote the employment judge. However, panels generally try to reach a consensus. For straightforward cases, the decision will be given orally that day, with written confirmation and fuller reasons communicated in writing a few days later if requested. A tribunal can delay making a decision in a more complex case.

Awards at employment tribunals

In an unfair dismissal claim the tribunal can order reinstatement or re-engagement, but this is very rarely done in practice. Even when tribunals make such an order, employers commonly refuse to implement it. If your employer refuses to comply, you have to apply again to the tribunal. It will probably award you additional compensation in such a situation.

If your employer still refuses to comply, you have to pursue the matter in a county court (sheriff court in Scotland). Ultimately, your employer cannot be forced to take you back, and the final remedy is compensation. If this cannot be recovered, you have to pursue the matter in the county court. Unfortunately, the costs of doing this often outweigh the benefit, although if your union is supporting you the cost will be to the union rather than you.

Most often the tribunal will order compensation to be paid. Table 1.1 shows the upper limits for compensation for the various types of claim. For discrimination claims, there is no upper limit and the compensation normally includes an element to cover hurt feelings. For unfair dismissal the upper limit is £78,335. For wrongful dismissal and breach of contract claims in the tribunals it is £25,000. These are upper limits, however, and usually compensation awarded is well below these levels.

Compensation for unfair dismissal includes an element to compensate for loss of earnings for the time between the dismissal and the tribunal decision. If you have got a new job, this element will be reduced to take account of what you are now being paid. The compensation will also reflect other losses, such as loss of pension rights.

The tribunal will also order a 'basic' award based on your length of service. As with a redundancy payment, the amount you get will depend on your length of service, how old you are and how much you are paid:

- For each complete year of employment after your 41st birthday you should get one and a half weeks' pay.

- For each complete year of employment after your 22nd birthday but before you turn 41 you should get one week's pay.

- For each complete year of employment below the age of 22 you should get half a week's pay.

There is an upper limit on the amount of a week's wage used to calculate the basic award, which is reviewed annually in line with the Retail Price Index. It is currently set at £475 a week, and the rate is reviewed (but not always increased) on 1 February each year.

In some circumstances, employers can be made to pay more compensation if they failed to let you use an internal disciplinary procedure. Similarly, your compensation may be reduced if you refused to use one. Your compensation can also be reduced if you are found to have contributed to your dismissal, or if your employer has already paid you some money, such as a redundancy payment.

Appeals

If you lose the case, you can request the tribunal to review its own decision. You must do this at the hearing or within 14 days of the decision being recorded. The grounds for doing this are limited. You would be likely to succeed, for example, if one of the parties was absent for part or all of the hearing or if new evidence unexpectedly became available, but not simply because you thought the decision was wrong.

An appeal is also possible to the employment appeal tribunal (EAT), which sits in London for England, Cardiff for Wales and Edinburgh for Scotland. The EAT is a special appeal tribunal that deals only with employment-related issues, nearly all on appeal from the employment tribunals. The appeal has to be lodged within 42 days of the date that the tribunal decision was sent to the parties (which appears on the last page of the judgement). A special form is required, which can be obtained from the employment tribunal office or directly from the EAT (see Chapter 9), and a £400 fee is payable (called a lodgement fee). The EAT will tell you what fee you must pay, when and how to pay it. Appeals are only allowed if the tribunal made a mistake or applied the law incorrectly, but this can include a 'perverse' decision by the tribunal, where, for example, the members did not understand the facts or came to a decision based on evidence that they hadn't seen. You will need to ask the tribunal for a copy of the full written reasons for its decision and in some cases a copy of the employment judge's notes. It is important to be properly represented by your union or by a solicitor. Unions may have in-house solicitors who will represent you or may engage a solicitor for you and pay the costs. Your employer can also appeal.

Leave

Jackie Kuti was granted extended leave to visit her family in Nigeria. Before she went she signed a document headed 'contractual letter for the provision of holiday entitlement'. This letter made clear that Jackie agreed to return to work on 28 September. It said: 'If you fail to do this your contract of employment will automatically terminate on that date.'

When Jackie returned to the UK on 26 September she fell ill and was unable to go back to work on the 28th. Her employers considered that her employment had ended automatically, as provided for in the letter, and wrote to tell her so.

Jackie claimed unfair dismissal. She lost at both a tribunal and the EAT. They ruled that the letter was quite clear and that Jackie had breached her undertaking to return to work.

But the Court of Appeal disagreed. It ruled that Jackie had been asked to sign away her legal rights to be protected against unfair dismissal. But the law is clear that you cannot give up legal rights this way (with the exception of the right to redundancy payments if you are on a fixed-term contract). Basically she had been asked to give up a right in return for an extended break.

This was an important test case. Following the judgement, employers cannot use 'automatic termination' clauses to get out of their duty to act reasonably in dismissal cases involving 'overstayers'. It is possible that similar 'automatic termination' clauses in other situations may also be found to be invalid on the same grounds.

Appeal from the EAT is to the Court of Appeal, but you need 'leave', or permission, from the EAT or Court of Appeal to do this. Appeal from the Court of Appeal is to the Supreme Court. You will certainly need legal representation at these stages.

It is also possible for a tribunal or any of the courts involved at an appeal stage to refer a case to the European Court of Justice. Only cases involving important legal principles that derive from EU law will go to Europe. It is likely to be a slow and expensive process, in which you will need the support of your union, a lawyer or an organization such as the Equality and Human Rights Commission.

It was not all right on the night

Jimmy Parker worked as a nightwatchman for his local council. He was sacked after being found absent from duty He had signed the book as if he had worked a whole shift up to 7 am, but was found at home in bed.

Jimmy said he had gone home because he was ill, but he was dismissed on the grounds that he had absented himself from his security duties without permission and without informing his superiors or making an appropriate entry in the message/incident book. A general warning had been issued to all nightwatchmen a few weeks earlier to the effect that deliberate absence from duty would lead to dismissal. Jimmy had worked for the council for 27 years and had a previously good record of service. At a tribunal hearing Jimmy won a case of unfair dismissal on the grounds that given his age and record of service dismissal was an unduly harsh penalty. However, the EAT reversed this decision. It said the council had acted reasonably because it had followed a fair procedure. Employees were aware of the consequences of such an action, and a proper appeals procedure had been exhausted.

As long as an employer follows a fair procedure it is up to the employer to decide whether or not to show leniency. It is not up to a tribunal to decide what it would have done in an employer's place. A clear message of cases like this is that, as long as employers stick to a procedure that is more or less in line with the Acas Code of Practice on Disciplinary and Grievance Procedures, they are within their rights to dismiss you as long as they apply the rules consistently, honour anything your contract of employment has to say about dismissal and do not discriminate.

Alternatives to tribunals and courts

There are various alternative ways of settling disputes with your employer that you should consider. Some of them will save you from having to pursue your claim in an employment tribunal or court.

You can reach a private agreement with your employer that they will pay you compensation, without them necessarily admitting liability (indeed, employers normally insist on this). An employer will also often require you to sign an agreement saying that you will drop the claim in return for the agreed compensation payment. You are best advised to negotiate such a deal with the help of a lawyer or a union.

A wiser option is to ask Acas to conciliate a formal agreement between you and the employer, known as a COT3. Acas does not charge for its conciliation services. By doing this, you agree to accept a stated sum of money as compensation to settle your claim(s). Once you have signed this, you will be barred from pursuing the claim(s) any further. Acas has a great deal of experience in these kinds of cases and can advise you on appropriate compensation amounts. This may be a particularly attractive option if you are not a union member and do not have the means to employ a solicitor to represent you at a hearing. A union may also advise you to go down this route.

It is now compulsory for you to notify Acas of your complaint before lodging a claim in the employment tribunal (see page 000 for more information).

A further option is to sign a 'settlement agreement', which is similar to a COT3 but need not involve Acas. It must be signed by you and the employer and a person specified as having authority to sign settlement agreements according to the Employment Rights (Dispute Resolution) Act 1998. This will be a solicitor, a trade union officer or a CAB worker who has an appropriate certificate of indemnity insurance. Again, once you have signed a settlement agreement you cannot pursue your claim(s) any further.

Acas also offers an arbitration scheme for unfair dismissal claims free of charge. If you and your employer agree to go to arbitration, Acas will appoint a qualified arbitrator, who will meet both of you in a formal hearing, probably but not necessarily in the workplace, hear both your arguments, listen to witnesses, look at relevant documents and then decide whether the dismissal was unfair. If the arbitrator decides that it was, he or she will order reinstatement, re-engagement or compensation exactly as tribunals do.

The scheme has real advantages. It is informal and quick and easier to represent yourself at, it will look primarily at the facts of the matter without having to refer to case law, and it is much more likely to award reinstatement or re-engagement than a tribunal. But there are also disadvantages. There is no right of appeal (although in exceptional circumstances judicial review may be available), and there are no lay members.

In general you should always take advice about which route is best for you in your particular circumstances. Your union or an advice agency, such as a CAB, should be able to help.

Sources of advice and representation

You do not need to be a qualified lawyer to represent somebody at a tribunal. Indeed, it is wholly unnecessary to involve lawyers in many cases. Recently a number of independent advisers have started to advertise their services in local papers and by other means. They offer to prepare your case and represent you at a tribunal for a fee and/or a cut of your compensation.

You should be extremely wary of such advisers. While some may be competent, you have absolutely no guarantee that they have any expertise. You should find out if their terms are reasonable. They may expect a very large share of any award you win. You should also discover their qualifications. Some claim that they have qualifications that they do not really have; others give themselves names such as 'legal advisers', which gives you the impression that they have some sort of legal qualification, when in reality this term means nothing.

The best support and representation you can have at an employment tribunal is probably either a trained trade union representative or a trade union lawyer. He or she will have considerable experience of how the tribunals work. He or she will also have a good understanding of common workplace issues and be able to spot errors made by your employer that another adviser would probably miss. Also, evidence shows that, in cases where the applicant is represented by a trade union, the applicant is more likely to settle and not progress to a full hearing.

If you are not a member of a union, you may be able to get free legal advice from a local law centre if there is one near you. Most larger towns and cities have them. Otherwise, Acas can provide advice, though not representation, as can staff at a CAB. If you do want to use a solicitor, make sure you choose one who has direct experience of employment tribunal representation, as solicitors often specialize in particular areas of the law. Someone who sold your house may have no experience of employment law.

Chapter Nine
Further information

In much of this book we have stressed the need to take further advice about your own particular circumstances if you have a problem at work. This chapter shows you where to find it.

Useful helplines and advice services

workSMART from the TUC

workSMART is the TUC's online information resource, providing up-to-date information and advice on your rights at work. It aims to become a one-stop shop for everything to do with working life. There is also a union-finder function if you want to find the right trade union to join (**www.worksmart.org.uk**).

The TUC website (**www.tuc.org.uk**) also contains employment rights advice and much up-to-date information about the world of work.

Acas

Acas, the Advisory, Conciliation and Arbitration Service, is a publicly funded body that promotes good workplace relations. Its website (**www.acas.org.uk**) contains a full range of information about employment rights and good practice. In addition, the Acas Helpline can provide advice to workers and employers on most of the rights-at-work issues covered in this book. The advice is free and confidential, and it provides a free translation service for over 100 languages. You can ask Acas about:

- employment rights and responsibilities;
- pay and the national minimum wage;
- discipline and grievance;
- contracts and terms and conditions;
- working time, rest breaks and holiday entitlement;
- equality in the workplace;
- working for an employment agency or gangmaster;
- agricultural workers' rights.

Tel: 0300 123 1100 (Monday to Friday, 8 am to 8 pm; Saturday, 9 am to 1 pm).

GOV.UK

The main government website www.gov.uk provides simple advice on all the basic employment rights, benefits and current rates of Statutory Sick Pay, redundancy pay and maternity pay. It will signpost you to other relevant and trustworthy sources of advice such as Acas and the Health and Safety Executive.

Enforcement of pay and work rights

Government enforcement agencies are responsible for enforcing some basic pay and work rights: HMRC's national minimum wage enforcement team; the Health and Safety Executive for working time rights; the Employment Agency Standards Inspectorate for agency workers' rights; and the Gangmasters Licensing Authority for workers in the agricultural and food processing sectors. The Acas Helpline can refer you on to these agencies, or you can make a complaint directly to them by completing a form that is available from **www.gov.uk**.

Employment tribunals

If you need information about making a claim or tribunal procedures you should call the Employment Tribunals Public Enquiry Line: 0300 123 1024 (England and Wales). 0141 354 8574 (Scotland). Textphone: 01509 221564 (Monday to Friday, 8.30 am to 5 pm).

The Employment Appeal Tribunal service is a non-departmental public body, whose primary role is to hear appeals from employment tribunals in England, Scotland and Wales. It also hears appeals from decisions of the Certification Officer and the Central Arbitration Committee, and has jurisdiction over certain industrial relations issues. Tel: 020 7273 1041 (Monday to Friday, 9 am to 4 pm); e-mail: londoneat@hmcts.gsi.gov.uk.

HM Revenue & Customs

HMRC offers a range of information on employment rights, tax and National Insurance contributions (NICs) for both employees and employers. It also has an online employment status indicator tool for tax and NICs purposes. See **www.hmrc.gov.uk** or **www.gov.uk**.

Redundancy

For information and advice on redundancy pay there is a Redundancy Payments Helpline: 0330 331 0020 (Monday to Friday, 9 am to 5 pm) or visit **www.gov.uk/redundancy-payments-helpline**.

Low pay units

Some parts of the country are covered by low pay units or similar bodies. These are voluntary organizations, not part of government.

Pay and Employment Rights Service (Yorkshire) Ltd
Tel: 01924 439381
www.pers.org.uk

Greater Manchester Pay and Employment Rights Advice Service
Tel: 0161 839 3888
**http://www.stockport.gov.uk/services/leisureculture/libraries/
libraryonline/ciss/gmpayandemploymentrightsadviceservice/**

Discrimination advice

The Equality and Human Rights Commission has a range of advice and guidance available online on discrimination law and equal pay and human rights: **www.equalityhumanrights.com**. The Equality and Advisory Support Service has replaced the EHRC's helpline for individuals. It can provide general advice on equality rights and signpost you to further help. Tel: 0808 800 0082; textphone: 0808 800 0084 (Monday to Friday, 9 am to 8 pm); **www.equalityadvisoryservice.com**.

Data protection

The Information Commissioner's Office (**www.ico.gov.uk**) is the UK's independent authority set up to uphold information rights in the public interest, promoting openness by public bodies and data privacy for individuals. It provides information and advice about the rights of individuals established under the Data Protection Act 1998 and the Freedom of Information Act 2000. Its helpline is on 0303 123 1113 (local rate) or 01625 545745 (national rate) (Monday to Friday, 9 am to 5 pm).

Whistle-blowing

Public Concern at Work (**www.pcaw.org.uk**) can provide advice for whistle-blowers on 020 7404 6609 or email: **whistle@pcaw.org.uk**.

Agency workers

The Recruitment and Employment Confederation (REC) on 020 7009 2144 or at **www.rec.uk.com** is the trade association for employment agencies. It sets standards for its members. If the agency you are employed by has an REC symbol on its premises or notepaper and you have a serious complaint about its behaviour, you can contact the REC, who may be able to investigate it on your behalf.

Health and safety

The Health and Safety Executive can help with health and safety and working time issues. It has a wide range of free leaflets, not just dealing with specific hazards but also providing help and advice for groups such as home workers or pregnant women. Most can also be viewed at **www.hse.gov.uk**.

Some issues are dealt with by the Environmental Health Department of your local council, including working time.

Working time

The Health and Safety Executive (see above) and the Environmental Health Department of your local council may be able to help and provide advice on your specific circumstances.

Family-friendly employment

Working Families (**www.workingfamilies.org.uk**) has a Parents and Carers Helpline for advice on rights at work: 0300 012 0312. Maternity Action (**www.maternityaction.org.uk**) also provides advice on maternity rights and has a helpline: 0845 600 8533.

The law and advice agencies

The Law Society (**www.lawsociety.org.uk**) is the national body for solicitors. It does not provide legal advice, and its helplines are only for solicitors. Members of the public should go to the Solicitors Regulation Authority (**www.sra.org.uk**), which can provide details of local solicitors who specialize in areas such as family law or personal injury. Its number is 0870 606 2555.

Law centres provide a free and independent professional legal service to disadvantaged people who live or work in their catchment areas. The Law Centres Federation will be able to tell you if you have a local law centre where you will be able to get free legal advice and possibly representation. Its website is **www.lawcentres.org.uk**, and it covers England, Wales and Northern Ireland, though there is also information on law centres in Scotland.

You can search for your local Citizens Advice Bureau (CAB) on the Citizens Advice website: **www.citizensadvice.org.uk**. Advice by phone is available from all Citizens Advice Bureaux. In addition, there is a national phone service for England (03444 111444) and Wales (03444 772020).

Tax credits and benefits

Information about how to apply for tax credits is available from **www.gov.uk**. You can get a claim form from the website or by calling the Tax Credits Office. Tel: 0345 300 3900; textphone: 0345 300 3909.

The Tax Credits Helpline provides general information about tax credits: 0345 300 3900 (Monday to Friday, 8 am to 8 pm; Saturday, 8 am to 4 pm).

There are a range of helplines available for those claiming disability benefits. See **www.gov.uk** for more information.

Criminal convictions

NACRO (National Association for the Care and Resettlement of Offenders), **www.nacro.org.uk**, helps over 39,000 ex-prisoners and offenders, with training or work and a place to live, to stop them reoffending. It has a resettlement helpline for individuals with a criminal record: 0300 123 1999 (Monday to Friday, 9 am to 5 pm) or helpline@nacro.org.uk.

Giving up smoking

QUIT (**www.quit.org.uk**) is a charity that helps smokers to stop and young people to never start. It offers a range of services including helplines and community programmes in eight different languages. It has a helpline: 0800 002200. The NHS provides an online advice service too: **www.nhs.uk/smokefree**.

Drugs

FRANK is the national drugs information service. It is a website and telephone helpline service offering advice, information and support to anyone concerned about drugs and solvent/volatile substance misuse, including drug misusers and their families, friends and carers. It offers free, confidential drugs information and advice 24 hours a day, seven days a week. Tel: 0300 123 6600; **www.talktofrank.com**.

Alcohol

Alcohol Concern (**www.alcoholconcern.org.uk**) provides advice on cutting down on drinking. If you are worried about your own or someone else's drinking you can contact their Drinkline: 0300 123 1110.

Britain's trade unions

If you want to join or contact a trade union, you can consult the workSMART website, **www.worksmart.org.uk**, which contains a union-finder to help you identify the most suitable union for you to join. The TUC's own site, **www.tuc.org.uk**, also has a union-finding page, publications to download and plenty of information on policy and current campaigns.

Jargon-buster

There is an even more comprehensive jargon-buster at **www.worksmart. org.uk**.

Acas   The Advisory, Conciliation and Arbitration Service is a publicly funded agency that provides advice to both employers and employees on industrial relations issues. It offers guidance, conciliation, mediation and arbitration upon request where there is a dispute between a worker, or a union, and an employer. It produces helpful codes of guidance on issues such as disciplinary procedures.

accident book   A book that must be provided in every workplace by the employer, in which all workplace accidents must be recorded.

accredited training   Training that is recognized by an official training organization.

additional adoption leave   The second period of 26 weeks' leave that you can take in addition to 26 weeks' ordinary adoption leave.

additional maternity leave (AML)   The second period of 26 weeks of maternity leave to which you are entitled on top of the 26 weeks of ordinary maternity leave. *NB:* Take care not to conflate the rules on leave and pay. All pregnant employees are entitled to 52 weeks' leave, divided into 26 weeks' OML and 26 weeks' AML, but only those who qualify will be entitled to Statutory Maternity Pay – paid for 39 weeks.

advances of wages   Some or all of your wages paid before you have done the work.

agency worker   Someone who gets a job through an employment agency, which will 'place' him or her with the hiring company; the agency *or* the hiring company will be the legal employer, depending on the terms set out in the contract between the worker, the hiring company and the agency. Usually agency workers work under the direct control of the hiring company.

annualized hours contract   A contract that specifies the normal number of hours to be worked over the period of a year (rather than a day or a week). This kind of arrangement can be used in sectors where there are seasonal fluctuations, such as making ice cream or Santa's grotto.

antenatal care   Care given to pregnant women (usually at clinics or hospitals but may include alternative treatments such as massage, acupuncture or attending yoga sessions) relating to their pregnancy (an appointment with the doctor for an issue that is not directly related to the pregnancy, such as a sprained ankle, would not count as antenatal care).

applicant A worker who has submitted a claim to an employment tribunal or someone who has applied for a job. Strictly speaking, the legal term is 'claimant'.

apprentice A specific legal term describing a person contractually bound to an employer to learn a trade or profession.

arbitration In arbitration, you and your employer allow an independent and impartial outsider (the arbitrator, or arbiter in Scotland) to determine the outcome of your problem. Arbitration differs from conciliation and mediation because the arbitrator acts like a judge, making a firm decision on a case.

assert a statutory right Ask an employer to give you something to which you are legally entitled, for example a written statement of employment particulars or to be paid the minimum wage.

associative discrimination Suffering less favourable treatment because of a 'protected characteristic' while not having that characteristic yourself. A claim may be brought by someone who is treated less favourably than others because he or she 'associates' with someone else who has the protected characteristic

back pay Wages or salary owed to you for work already performed.

bonuses Extra money for good performance, high productivity etc.

breach of contract When either you or your employer breaks, or ignores, the terms agreed in your contract of employment, either express or implied.

career break schemes Periods of leave, paid or unpaid, offered by an employer for employees to pursue other activities; usually only allowed after you have been employed by that employer for a set period of time.

casual worker A worker who is only employed when work is available, usually either on a temporary contract or on call when required to do a particular job or provide a service.

civil courts Courts that deal with non-criminal issues, for example matrimonial issues, commercial disputes and employment law.

claimant A worker who has submitted a claim to an employment tribunal.

collective agreement An agreement between a trade union and an employer on behalf of a specified group of workers, usually relating to their pay and other working conditions.

comparator A legal term used in discrimination cases – another worker doing a job comparable to your own.

compromise agreement A legally binding agreement in which the employee agrees to waive his or her rights to pursue claims against his or her employer in a tribunal or court in exchange for compensation. To be valid it must satisfy certain legal conditions, and the employee must have received independent advice on its terms and effect from a solicitor, a designated trade union officer or a designated advice bureau worker.

conciliation   Similar to mediation. Both words describe the same process, but conciliation is normally used when there is a potential or actual claim to an employment tribunal, rather than more general employment problems.

constructive dismissal   Where you leave a job because your employer has breached the terms (implied or express) of your contract of employment, eg refused to pay you, or bullied or harassed you, or because the working conditions have become so bad that you cannot continue. You resign in response to the employer's breach and claim that you have been constructively dismissed. Claims are made in the employment tribunal or civil court.

continuity of service   Having worked for the same employer (in some cases different employers in the same sector) for a continuous period of time, ignoring breaks for maternity, sickness, holidays and some other temporary interruptions.

contract worker   Someone employed on a short-term contract, usually to do a particular job. The contract will normally state when the employment will finish.

costs   When a court orders you to pay the legal costs incurred by the winning party, or when your costs are paid by the losing party.

COT3   A form used by Acas to record an agreement between you and your employer to settle a claim either before or after the claim has been lodged in the employment tribunal.

crown servant   Some civil servants and government employees, who may have special terms and conditions of employment.

custom and practice   Something that has been done in a particular way, consistently, over a long period of time. In employment law your terms and conditions may change by custom and practice. For example, for the past 20 years an employer has allowed staff to go home early on Christmas Eve. All staff have come to expect this, and the employer feels obliged to allow it to continue. A court may decide that this has now been included in your contract of employment by custom and practice.

damages   Compensation when your employer causes you harm, either physical or in terms of your career prospects, injury to feelings etc.

dependant   Your parent, wife, husband or child, or someone else living with you as part of your household; an elderly neighbour who relies on your care may be defined as a dependant.

detriment   A legal term used to describe action taken by your employer against you unfairly, other than sacking you, such as refusing you training or promotion because you are in a trade union.

direct discrimination   A legal term meaning treating someone less favourably (than others are or would be treated) because of a 'protected characteristic'.

directive   A piece of European Union law that applies in the UK.

disciplinary hearing   A formal hearing organized by your employer where you are required to attend and answer for unsatisfactory performance or conduct.

disclosure of documents   A legal term used when an employment tribunal requires you or your employer to exchange documents that you intend to refer to at the hearing, for example timesheets.

dismiss/dismissal   Legal term for sack, or termination of your employment.

duty of care   Employers owe you a duty of care. This means that they are responsible for ensuring that you are cared for at work and do not have to work in unsafe or unhealthy conditions. This can include protection against bullying or stress. An implied duty of care exists in all contracts of employment.

effective date of termination   The date on which your employment ends, ie at the end of the notice period, the date on which your contract expires or the last day that you worked.

employee   In law someone employed under a 'contract of employment', giving him or her a number of statutory and contractual rights.

employment status   The legal definition of whether you are a 'worker', an 'employee' or 'self-employed'.

employment tribunals   Special courts of law that hear employment cases, for example sex discrimination, unfair dismissal, or non-payment of the national minimum wage.

ET1   An application form on which you make a claim to an employment tribunal.

express terms   Terms that are written in a contract of employment, for example the amount you are to be paid.

final written warning   A final stage in a disciplinary procedure at work, after which you can be dismissed.

fixed-term contract   A contract of employment that expires on a date specified in the contract.

flexible working   A broad concept that allows employees to adapt their working hours, times and even place of work to suit their lifestyles and caring responsibilities. People with childcare or caring responsibilities who meet the eligibility criteria have the legal right to have their request for flexible working considered by their employers.

full-time There is no precise definition in UK law but generally considered to be working 35 hours a week or more.

further and better particulars A legal term – meaning 'a request to provide more (detailed) information'. For example, a woman claiming sex discrimination may be asked to provide further information (than has already been provided) on the discriminatory way in which she was treated by the employer.

gender reassignment A personal, social and sometimes medical process by which a person's gender presentation (the way the person appears to others) is changed. Anyone who proposes, starts or has completed a process to change his or her gender is protected from discrimination under the Equality Act 2010.

grievance A legal term meaning concerns, problems or complaints that employees raise with their employer. The complaint will normally be put in writing. There is a legal requirement for employers to have a grievance procedure.

gross salary or wages Wages before tax and National Insurance and other deductions, and including any other elements, eg performance-related pay

guarantee payment The minimum amount payable to you by your employer if you are laid off, or told to go home until work becomes available.

harassment Behaviour that violates your dignity or creates an intimidating, hostile, degrading, humiliating or offensive environment for you, and that is linked to 'protected characteristics'.

implied terms Terms that are not written into your contract of employment but are considered to be part of it, for example a duty to provide a healthy and safe working environment for you.

incapacity Usually, medical reasons why you cannot work.

indirect discrimination A type of discrimination that arises when an employer unjustifiably applies to everyone a 'provision, criterion or practice' that disadvantages employees who share a 'protected characteristic' and that disadvantages you. For example, a new shift pattern that means everyone has to work until 10 pm would disadvantage those employees with caring responsibilities, ie mainly women. Because of your childcare responsibilities you cannot work until 10 pm, so unless the employer can justify the new shift pattern it will be indirectly discriminatory.

insolvency When an employer is officially declared bankrupt.

itemized pay statement A pay statement showing how your pay is made up. It will include terms such as basic pay, overtime, performance-related pay, holidays etc.

lay members   The non-legal-side members of an employment tribunal.

legal precedent   A ruling made in a court or appeals tribunal, which then influences future cases involving similar issues, often set by a 'test case'.

Maternity Allowance   Benefit paid to pregnant women or new mothers in some circumstances.

maternity certificate (MAT B1)   A certificate issued by your doctor or midwife confirming your pregnancy and the expected week of childbirth.

maternity leave   Time off work for pregnancy and childbirth.

mediation   An independent and impartial third party discusses the issues in dispute with you and your employer. This is sometimes done separately, sometimes together with a view to helping you both come up with an acceptable solution. Mediation is voluntary, so both you and your employer must agree to become involved. A mediator cannot impose his or her solution; you and your employer must both agree to it.

national minimum wage   The least that you must be paid an hour.

notice of dismissal   A letter, or sometimes a verbal statement, from your employer telling you that they intend to dismiss you on a certain date.

notice pay/payment in lieu of notice   You may agree to accept payment of wages for your notice period instead of continuing to work until your date of dismissal.

notified day of return   The date on which you tell your employer you will return after taking maternity, adoption or paternity leave.

occupational pension   A pension scheme provided by your employer (as opposed to the state pension or any private pension you have); you may or may not have to contribute to your occupational pension.

on call   Available to work if required (typically social workers, security staff etc).

ordinary adoption leave   This is the first 26 weeks' leave to which you are entitled if you are adopting a child.

ordinary maternity leave (OML)   The initial 26 weeks of maternity leave to which all employees are entitled.

out of time   Missing the deadline for submitting a complaint to an employment tribunal.

overtime   Hours worked over and above those specified in your contract.

parental leave   Unpaid leave of 18 weeks in total per child, which can be used up to the child's 18th birthday, with a limit of four weeks a year per child.

part-time   There is no legal definition but generally anyone working fewer hours than full-time staff.

passive smoking   Being exposed to other people's smoke.

paternity leave Two weeks' paid leave for fathers of either a newborn baby or an adopted child who meet the eligibility criteria.

perception discrimination Direct discrimination also covers discrimination because of perception, for example if a man is refused the opportunity for promotion because he is wrongly perceived to be gay. Perception discrimination does not apply to pregnancy and maternity or marriage and civil partnership.

perverse decision A legal term meaning a decision that no normal or rational person would have made.

positive action Actions by employers allowed under the Equality Act 2010 in order to support and advance equality for employees who may be under-represented in the workplace, experience disadvantage or have different needs that relate to a 'protected characteristic'.

postponement Legal term used when a tribunal puts off concluding a hearing, or starting a hearing, until a future date.

pre-hearing review Part of an employment tribunal procedure, when the chair hears the basic details of a case and decides whether or not it is strong enough to proceed.

preliminary hearing Part of an employment tribunal procedure in which the tribunal will decide a preliminary qualifying issue, for example whether or not you are an 'employee' in the legal sense and can proceed with your case.

prohibited conduct The UK discrimination laws now share a common approach and similar definitions. The law generally prohibits certain kinds of actions, known as 'prohibited conduct'. These are direct discrimination, indirect discrimination, discrimination arising from disability and failure to make reasonable adjustments (applies to disability only), harassment and victimization.

protected characteristics You have the right not to be discriminated against at work because of your age, disability, gender reassignment, marriage or civil partnership status, pregnancy or maternity, race, religion or belief, sex or sexual orientation. The law refers to these categories or groups as 'protected characteristics'.

protective award Employment tribunal compensation award – usually 90 days' pay – to an employee dismissed for redundancy in circumstances where the employer had failed to consult with employee representatives, eg trade union representatives.

qualifying period A legal term meaning the length of time you have been working for your employer in order to qualify for certain rights; for example, you must have normally worked for one year (two years from 6 April 2012) at least before you can claim unfair dismissal.

reasonable adjustments   Under the Equality Act 2010, an employer is required to take all reasonable steps to remove the disadvantage facing disabled employees in the workplace. This can include making certain adaptations to the working environment to allow a disabled worker to work for them, for example installing a hearing loop facility.

recognize   The formal term for an agreement to negotiate certain workplace issues, for example pay or health and safety, with a trade union.

redundant/redundancy   When there is no longer the requirement for a job; the term 'redundant' specifically applies to the job and not to the individual doing it.

re-engagement   Returning to work for the same employer in a different job.

reference   Usually a written, but sometimes verbal, report by a past employer, or from a school or college, or a responsible impartial adult, about the abilities of a job applicant to do the job for which he or she is applying, or a statement about how the applicant did his or her previous job.

reinstatement   Being restored to your previous job after a dismissal.

resign   Leave your job.

respondent   The employer against whom a claim is being made at an employment tribunal.

retired   No longer working, usually because of age but sometimes illness.

RSI   Repetitive strain injury: an injury or condition caused by doing the same thing over and over again at work, eg word processing.

self-certification form   When you take time off sick, for the first period you write a letter to your employer saying that you were off for whatever reason.

self-employed   Not contractually bound to an employer as 'an employee', though you may be contracted to provide a service to them; usually paying your tax and National Insurance yourself.

severance payment   This is not a precise legal term in the UK. Normally it refers to a payment made to you by an employer in return for you agreeing to leave without pursuing a claim against your employer.

sexual orientation   Your sexuality.

shared parental leave   Maternity or adoption leave shared between partners with responsibility for a child.

split shifts   Working part of a shift, then taking time off and then resuming work. An example might be working in a pub or restaurant for four hours over lunchtime and then working another four hours in the evening.

staff handbook   Explains how the company operates, its aims and objectives and, usually, general terms and conditions of employment. It may be given to you when you start work, and all or part is likely to be a legal document if it sets out some of your terms and conditions.

Statutory Adoption Pay   The minimum you must be paid during your adoption leave if you satisfy the conditions for payment.

Statutory Maternity Pay   The minimum you must be paid during 39 weeks of your maternity leave if you satisfy the conditions for payment.

Statutory Paternity Pay   The minimum you must be paid during your two weeks of ordinary paternity leave if you satisfy the conditions for payment.

Statutory Sick Pay   The minimum you must be paid when you are off sick.

suspension   When you are sent home from work, usually prior to any disciplinary action being taken, often on full pay, pending an investigation into allegations made regarding your conduct.

temporary workers   Those engaged for a short time, or to do a particular job.

terms of your contract   What your contract says about your conditions of work; terms are legally binding on you and your employer once you have started working under them, and by doing so you have agreed to them.

transfer of undertakings   When a business changes owners, or an activity moves from the public to the private sector.

unauthorized deduction from wages   Money taken out of your wages without your permission and without it saying in your contract that it may be done.

unfair dismissal   Legal term for a dismissal carried out other than for a potentially fair reason or without going through an agreed company procedure for dismissals.

unmeasured work   Work by workers who have fixed tasks but no fixed hours of work, eg hostel wardens or domestic workers.

verbal warning   Usually part of a disciplinary procedure, a first warning, to be followed by a further warning, probably written, if you do not improve your performance or stop doing something wrong.

victimization   When someone is treated unfavourably after complaining about or alleging discrimination or harassment or agreeing to be a witness in a case for someone else who has made a complaint.

visual display units (VDUs)   Computer screens.

void   Legal term meaning a term in a contract that is not valid, for example if your contract states that you will be paid less than the national minimum wage.

waive   A legal term meaning to agree to do without something.

whistle-blower   Someone who makes a complaint about malpractice in the workplace. In some circumstances you are legally protected against detrimental action taken by your employer as a result.

witness order   A legal term meaning an order in a court or tribunal to require a witness in a case to attend court or produce a statement.

worker   A legal term that goes wider than employee. The difference is that an employee either has or is entitled to a contract of employment. Someone who is a worker but not an employee works for someone else but usually on the basis of providing a service. Strictly speaking, all employees are workers, but not all workers are employees. In practice, however, worker is often used to describe those who are not employees.

written statement of employment particulars   A legal document, not strictly speaking a contract, in which your basic terms and conditions of employment are set out. However, your contract of employment may include your written statement.

written statement of reasons for dismissal   A legal term for a letter from your employer stating why you have been dismissed.

written warning   Usually the middle or final part of a disciplinary procedure, in which you are told that if you do not improve you will be disciplined or dismissed.

wrongful dismissal   A legal term meaning that your employment has been terminated in a way that does not follow the procedures in, or in some other way goes against, your contract of employment. A common example is not getting enough notice.

zero-hours contract   A contract of employment where the employer is not obliged to provide work for you and, if work is offered, you are not obliged to accept it. The contract does not specify your hours and states that when you are not required to work you will not be paid.

Index

Page numbers in *italic* indicate figures or table